Bloom's Modern Critical Views

Bloom's Modern Critical Views

AFRICAN-AMERICAN POETS
Volume 2: 1950s to the Present
New Edition

Edited and with an introduction by
Harold Bloom
Sterling Professor of the Humanities
Yale University

BLOOM'S
LITERARY CRITICISM
An imprint of Infobase Publishing

Bloom's Modern Critical Views: African-American Poets: Volume 2—New Edition
Copyright © 2010 by Infobase Publishing
Introduction © 2010 by Harold Bloom

Bloom's Literary Criticism
An imprint of Infobase Publishing
132 West 31st Street
New York NY 10001

Library of Congress Cataloging-in-Publication Data
African-American poets. Volume 2 / edited and with an introduction by Harold Bloom. — New ed.
    p. cm. — (Bloom's modern critical views)
    Includes bibliographical references and index.
    ISBN 978-1-60413-810-8 (alk. paper)
    1. American poetry—African American authors—History and criticism. 2. African Americans—Intellectual life. 3. African Americans in literature. I. Bloom, Harold.
    PS310.N4A356 2010
    811'.5409896073—dc22
    [B]
                                    2010005017

Bloom's Literary Criticism books are available at special discounts when purchased in bulk quantities for businesses, associations, institutions, or sales promotions. Please call our Special Sales Department in New York at (212) 967-8800 or (800) 322-8755.

You can find Bloom's Literary Criticism on the World Wide Web at
http://www.chelseahouse.com

Contributing editor: Pamela Loos
Cover designed by Takeshi Takahashi
Composition by IBT Global, Troy NY
Cover printed by IBT Global, Troy NY
Book printed and bound by IBT Global, Troy NY
Date printed: June 2010
Printed in the United States of America

10 9 8 7 6 5 4 3 2 1

This book is printed on acid-free paper.

All links and Web addresses were checked and verified to be correct at the time of publication. Because of the dynamic nature of the Web, some addresses and links may have changed since publication and may no longer be valid.

Contents

Editor's Note

My introduction centers on, at the exclusion of many others, four poets vital to the development of contemporary African-American poetry.

Audrey T. McCluskey explores the cultural and religious sensibilities informing the work of Lucille Clifton, after which William J. Harris assesses the democratic appeal of Nikki Giovanni's writing.

Max W. Thomas presents the work of Carl Phillips and Reginald Shepherd, by way of Christopher Marlowe and the pastoral tradition, followed by Elizabeth Dodd's perusal of the ecological scope of Michael S. Harper's poetry.

Zofia Burr visits the presidential inaugural stage and Maya Angelou's embodiment of oral tradition, after which Malin Pereira frames the early work of Rita Dove within her cosmopolitanist influences.

Angela M. Salas broaches the negative capabilities of Yusef Komunyakaa, followed by James Smethurst's appraisal of the ways traditionally black colleges served as essential staging grounds for a burgeoning African-American poetics.

The volume concludes with two emerging voices in the tradition. Rick Benjamin traces the American idiom informing the work of Kevin Young, and Annette Debo delves into Natasha Trethewey's historical sequence, *Bellocq's Ophelia*.

HAROLD BLOOM

Introduction

I will write here only briefly about four vital poets: Robert Hayden, Derek
Walcott, Jay Wright, and Thylias Moss. This is not to evade my authentic admiration for aspects of the work of Gwendolyn Brooks, Michael S.
Harper, Ishmael Reed, Yusef Komunyakaa, Rita Dove, Carl Phillips, Elizabeth Alexander, and others.

1

Robert Hayden was a major poet, who was schooled by W. H. Auden, a
teacher's legacy still evident in poems as distinguished as "The Islands":

> Always this waking dream of palmtrees,
> magic flowers—of sensual joys
> like treasures brought up from the sea.
>
> Always this longing, this nostalgia
> for tropic islands we
> have never known and yet recall.
>
> We look for ease upon these islands named
> to honor holiness; in their chromatic
> torpor catch our breath.
>
> Scorn greets us with promises of rum,
> hostility welcomes us to bargain sales.
> We make friends with Flamboyant trees.

I hear Auden, at his most persuasive, in: "We look for ease upon those islands we / have never known and yet recall." But Hayden's authentic agon was with Hart Crane, whose high rhetoric of vision underlies the astonishing "Middle Passage" and "Runagate Runagate," which achieve a sublime that only Jay Wright among Hayden's followers was able to attain:

> Shuttles in the rocking loom of history,
> the dark ships move, the dark ships move,
> their bright ironical names
> like jests of kindness on a murderer's mouth;
> plough through thrashing glister toward
> fata morgana's lucent melting shore,
> weave toward New World littorals that are
> mirage and myth and actual shore.

Hart Crane would have loved this opening octave of "Middle Passage," III. Hayden, already fully formed in "Middle Passage" and "Runagate," reached his ecstatic originality in chants like "Bone-Flower Elegy," with its fierce conclusion:

> I whisper but shrink from the arms
> that would embrace me
> and treading water reach
> arched portals opening on a desert
> groves of enormous nameless flowers
> twist up from firegold sand
> skull flowers flowers of sawtooth bone
> their leaves and petals interlock
> caging me for you beastangel
> raging toward me
> angelbeast shining come
> to rend me and redeem

In this dream vision, the dead beloved is invoked with triumphant ambivalences and with a sadomasochistic exultation that scares me with its intensity. Robert Hayden was so strong a poet that the wounds he inflicts tend to endure.

2

The West Indian poet Derek Walcott, a Nobel laureate, also started from Auden, but like Hayden's attachment to Hart Crane's mode, Walcott became most himself when he explored his affinity to Wallace Stevens, as here in the majestic poem "The Bounty":

> The mango trees serenely rust when they are in flower,
> nobody knows the name for that voluble cedar
> whose bell-flowers fall, the pomme-arac purples its floor.
>
> The blue hills in late afternoon always look sadder.
> The country night waiting to come in outside the door;
> the firefly keeps striking matches, and the hillside fumes
>
> with a bluish signal of charcoal, then the smoke burns
> into a larger question, one that forms and unforms,
> then loses itself in a cloud, till the question returns.

But again like Hayden, Walcott does not wear a secondhand suit of clothes (as did such celebrated modern American poets as Archibald MacLeish, John Peale Bishop, and Robert Lowell). Walcott's highest rhetoric is neither Audenesque nor Stevensian but very much his own:

> I tracked them where they led across the street
> to the bright side, entering the wax-
> sealed smell of neon, human heat,
> some all-night diner with its wise-guy cook,
> his stub thumb in my bowl of stew, and one
> man's pulped and beaten face, its look
> acknowledging all that, white-dark outside,
> was possible: some beast prowling the block,
> something fur-clotted, running wild
> beyond the boundary of will. Outside,
> more snow had fallen. My heart charred.
> I longed for darkness, evil that was warm.
> Walking, I'd stop and turn. What had I heard
> wheezing behind my heel with whitening breath?
> Nothing. Sixth Avenue yawned wet and wide.
> The night was white. There was nowhere to hide.

3

I want only to make a brief but large estimate of Wright's achievement, now fully available in his *Transfigurations: Collected Poems* (2000). I have reread, studied, and taught Wright for decades, and I find him comparable to the great masters of the sublime mode: Hölderlin, Hart Crane, Luis Cernuda, Paul Celan. Like them, Jay Wright is a difficult and demanding poet, and again, with them, he is a permanent poet.

4

Thylias Moss is a poet who perpetually delights and astonishes me, with a wit comparable to that of the Canadian poet Anne Carson. Her hallucinatory force is difficult to describe, her originality being so enormous. Here is the second verse paragraph of her "The Undertaker's Daughter Feels Neglect":

> It's been years since the mailman came, years
> since I woke in the middle of the night
> thinking a party was going on downstairs,
> thinking my father was a magician
> and all those scantily clad women his assistants,
> wondering why no one could hear me,
> why I made to disappear permanently in the box.
> I seldom wake at all anymore.

The grisly delight of this is infectious: Read the poem aloud to someone else. To be the daughter of an undertaker-magician who specializes in beautiful female—shall we say assistants, or shall we say corpses?—ought not to be a hilarious fate, but Thylias Moss renders it so. Her wit and invention being supreme, I will venture no prophecies on her poems to come.

AUDREY T. MCCLUSKEY

Tell the Good News:
A View of the Works of Lucille Clifton

"Lucille Clifton was born in Depew, New York, in 1969. She attended Howard University and Fredonia State Teachers' College. She now lives in Baltimore with her husband and their six children. Mrs. Clifton also writes children's books."

Four sparse sentences[1] constitute most of what has been written as a biographical and critical statement about Lucille Clifton and her work. The lack of critical attention afforded this writer who has been steadily producing poetry and books for children for well over a decade is a major oversight in literary criticism.

We can only guess at the reasons. Lucille Clifton is a soft-spoken poet. She writes verse that does not leap out at you, nor shout expletives and gimmicks to gain attention. A public poet whose use of concrete symbols and language is easily discernible, Lucille Clifton is guided by the dictates of her own consciousness rather than the dictates of form, structure, and audience. She is not an "intellectual" poet, although she does not disdain intellect. She simply prefers to write from her heart. Her poetry is concrete, often witty, sometimes didactic, yet it can be subtle and understated. Her short-lined economical verse is often a grand mixture of simplicity and wisdom. Repeated readings of her work show her to be a poet in control of her material and one who is capable of sustaining a controlling idea with seemingly little effort.

From *Black Women Writers (1950–1980)*, pp. 139–49. © 1984 by Mari Evans.

Clifton is a poet of a literary tradition which includes such varied poets as Walt Whitman, Emily Dickinson, and Gwendolyn Brooks, who have inspired and informed her work.

Lucille Clifton writes with conviction; she always takes a moral and hopeful stance. She rejects the view that human beings are pawns in the hands of whimsical fate. She believes that we can shape our own destiny and right the wrongs by taking a moral stand.

> I [always] wanted to make things better.
> I wanted to make things right. I always
> thought I was supposed to.[2]

Lucille Clifton's belief in her ability (and ours) to make things better and her belief in the concept of personal responsibility pervade her work. These views are especially pronounced in her books for children.

Her children's books are her most prolific literary product, and no analysis of her work could ignore their overall importance. Her books for children introduce themes, ideas and points of view that may sometimes find their way into her poetry. It is important to note that she does not greatly alter her style as she moves from one genre to another. Her language remains direct, economical, and simply stated. She does not patronize the children for whom she writes. She gives them credit for being intelligent human beings who do not deserve to be treated differently because of their age. Being the mother of six children must certainly give her material for her books, but it is her respect for children as people and her finely tuned instincts about what is important to them—their fears, their joys—that make her a successful writer of children's literature.

One of her favorite characters in her books for children is Everett Anderson. He is a boy of six or seven, living with his working mother, who teaches him responsibility, pride, and love. He is reminded to "walk tall" in the world and to be proud of who he is. He is always referred to by his complete name, which helps to underscore his sense of identity and belonging. Yet Everett Anderson does not exist in a world of bliss and fantasy. He experiences periods of loneliness—when he remembers the good times that he had with his Daddy when he lived with them—and frustration—when he wants to bake a cake but finds that "the sugar is almost gone and payday's not 'til later on."[3] He will survive these momentary frustrations because he feels secure and loved.

> Being six
> is full of tricks
> and Everett Anderson knows it

> Being a boy
> is full of joy
> And Everett Anderson shows it.[4]

The understated message in the Everett Anderson books is that a loving, caring environment more than makes up for any real or perceived deprivations when it comes to the development of a positive self-concept. Everett Anderson seems to understand that.

> Thank you for the things we have,
> thank you for Mama and turkey and fun,
> thank you for Daddy wherever he is,
> thank you for me, Everett Anderson.[5]

The importance of a nurturing family in the teaching of a positive self-concept is illustrated at another level in *Good, Says Jerome*, a book about a little boy, Jerome, who is overcome with worry and self-doubt when he learns that the family will be moving to a new place. He is helped to deal with this trauma by an older sister who patiently explains some of the facts of life to him, including the meaning of Black:

> Black is a color
> like yellow or white
> It's got nothing to do
> with wrong or right
> It's a feeling inside
> about who we are and
> how strong and free.[6]

Clifton is very cognizant of the fears that are ignited by a child's imagination. Her books are written to help give reassurance. She delicately treats both the pains and joys of childhood in order to help children accept both emotions as part of the unique experience of being who they are. In Clifton's books for children, self-love, and self-acceptance is the message. An example of this message is summarized in *The Black BC's*, a collection of rhymes depicting Black history and the Black experience.

> N is for natural
> or real or true
> the you of yourself
> and the self of you[7]

In her poetry, Clifton continues to advocate that Black children be taught self-worth and encouraged to develop the mental and spiritual toughness that they will require to survive in a society that is hostile to their development. In the following poem, the children are called upon to make decisions for themselves and to begin to take control of their lives. They must become socially responsible—for they shall someday lead.

Come home from the movies
Black girls and boys.
The picture be over and the screen
be cold as our neighborhood.
Come home from the show,
don't be the show . . .
Show our fathers how to walk like men,
they already know how to dance.[8]

The movies serve as a metaphor for the fantasies and falseness in society that stunt our children's growth. She believes that what is important in life is found, not in the movies but in the values that are passed through generations.

we have always loved each other
children   all ways
Pass it on.[9]

Clifton's view of herself as a writer is based, in part, upon her belief that "things don't fall apart. Things hold. Lines connect in ways that last and last and lives become generations made out of pictures and words just kept."[10] She is interested in the continuity of experience and the writer's unique ability to connect generations of people and to remind them who they are and from whence they came.

As a poet, her connections include the works of other poets such as Emily Dickinson, Walt Whitman, and Gwendolyn Brooks, who serve as literary predecessors for many of her concerns. Like that of Emily Dickinson and Gwendolyn Brooks, Clifton's work is heavily influenced by Christian optimism. To these poets, the world is defined by possibility. Also, like Emily Dickinson and Gwendolyn Brooks, Clifton prefers to experience life through her senses, producing a poetry that is not devoid of wonder and ebullience. Like her predecessors, Clifton can marvel at nature and find worthy themes in everyday and commonplace occurrences. Clifton's short elliptical verse, her simultaneous acknowledgment of pain and possibility, and her use of domestic images are especially Dickinsonian. "I Am Not Done Yet" is a poem which highlights these comparisons.[11]

Also like Emily Dickinson, Clifton finds joy in "not having" and in being out of step with public opinion.[12]

The preference for "our no place" over "houses straight as / dead men" is a rejection of established opinion and an assertion of an independent view of reality. She seems to relish being different and is not concerned that others may consider her odd. In her poem "Admonitions," she tells her children how to deal with it.

> Children
> When they ask you
> why your mama so funny
> say she is a poet
> she don't have no sense.[13]

Among her identifiable predecessors, it is Gwendolyn Brooks with whom Mrs. Clifton shares her racial and spiritual legacy. Although her poetry does not contain the variety of form and experimentation or breadth of subject matter found in the poetry of Gwendolyn Brooks, they share a sensibility rooted in the Black experience and in Christian idealism. The religious values translate into poems that value simplicity, despise injustice, and identify with the common, uncelebrated man and woman. Lucille Clifton, like Gwendolyn Brooks, gives identity and substance to the everyday people in her poems by giving them names, and therefore a history, such as "Willie B.," "Tyrone," and "Everett Anderson."

The Black experience is depicted in Mrs. Clifton's poems, not by proclamation but through a nurtured sensibility that is rendered in language, substance and feeling. The poem "Good Times" illustrates these qualities

> My Daddy has paid the rent
> and the insurance man is gone
> and the light is back on
> and my uncle Brud has hit
> for one dollar straight
> and they is good times
> good times
> good times[14]

Clifton's feminine sensibility, like her Blackness, runs deep. The femaleness in her poems—children, family, domesticity, and the concerns of the ordinary woman—derive not from a newly spawned feminine consciousness but from historical role models of Black, keeping-on women who are her inspiration.

> Harriet
> if i be you
> let me not forget
> to be the pistol
> pointed
> to be the madwoman
> at the river's edge
> warning
> to be free or die[15]

This poem merges a collective and personal past and serves to renew the speaker's acceptance of the challenges faced by her ancestors.

The female voice in Clifton's poetry is her most sustained and her most introspective. Her female poems reflect her personal journey toward self-discovery and reconciliation. She traces her origins to the Dahomey woman who was the founder of Clifton's family in America. Mammy Ca'line is the link with Africa and a lost-found past. In "Ca'line's Prayer," Mammy Ca'line speaks through the poet, whose function is to keep alive the aching memory and to pass on her cry for redemption.

> Remember me from Wydah
> Remember the child
> running across Dahomey
> black as ripe papaya
> juicy as sweet berries
> and set me in the rivers of your glory.
> Ye Ma Jah.[16]

At birth, the weight of this history is passed on to the poet, who inherits not only Mammy Ca'line's discontent, but the legacy of her namesake—her grandmother Lucille—the first Black woman legally lynched in the state of Virginia.[17]

> . . . who waited by the crossroads
> in Virginia
> and shot the whiteman off his horse,
> killing the killer of sons.

light breaks from her life
to her lives ...

mine already is
an Afrikan name.[18]

The "light" that she inherits is an avenging light that is activated by the special circumstances of her birth.

i was born in a hotel,
a maskmaker
my bones were knit by
a perilous knife.
my skin turned round
at midnight and
i entered the earth in
a woman jar.[19]

By saying yes to her legacy, Clifton acknowledges a responsibility to the Dahomey women who have preceded her and to all unsung Black warriors who await vindication.

The unsung, the unvindicated for whom the poet speaks include those like "Miss Rosie," whom society has cast aside.

... wrapped up like garbage
sitting, surrounded by the smell
of too old potato peels

... sitting, waiting for your mind
like next week's grocery

... you wet brown bag of a woman
who used to be the best looking gal in Georgia[20]

The poem emanates from a fusion of language and meaning. The language denotes highly charged sensory images of an old woman discarded by society and left to rot like garbage. The theme of human waste and uselessness is suggested throughout the poem by the placement of key words and phrases like "sitting," "waiting for your mind" and metaphors like "too old potato peels" and "wet brown bag of a woman." The tragedy of Miss Rosie's present state is heightened by the knowledge that she "used to be called the Georgia

Rose—the best looking gal in Georgia." Although she is the commanding presence in the poem, this poem is not only about the destruction of Miss Rosie; it also conveys the speaker's resolve to fight the forces that caused that human waste and suffering. "I stand up," the speaker says, "through your destruction. I stand up."

The tenacious spirit and resolve of the speaker in "Miss Rosie" is also the theme of the poem "For deLawd." It is a poem which seeks to merge the speaker's individual optimism and faith with a larger, well-articulated historical tradition of women who, under adverse circumstances fought the good fight and just kept on pushing. The speaker has inherited her mantle and thus proclaims:

> ... I got a long memory
> and I came from a line
> of black and going on women.[21]

This poem is another illustration of Clifton's belief in the continuity of human experience and in our indebtedness to the generations that preceded us.

The "going on" women that Clifton writes about are like their counterparts in blues songs. They know that the world is not a sane and rational place, but it is the only world that we have. So they have learned to manipulate the chaos—not to control it—to ensure their individual and collective survival. This cold reality of that statement can force undesirable alternatives, as in "The Lost Baby Poem," a poem in which a mother speaks to the unmade child that poverty has forced her to abort. As in a blues song, she only wants to explain to her lost baby the *necessity* of her actions.

> You would have been born into winter
> in the year of the disconnected gas
> and no car we would have made the thin
> walk over Genesee hill into Canada wind
> to watch you slip like ice into strangers' hands
> you would have fallen naked as snow into winter.[22]

"The Lost Baby Poem" is also structured like a blues song in three parts, with a statement, an embellishment, and a resolution or rebuttal. It is one of Clifton's most lyrical poems. The longer length allows for the development of sustained images and for the use of extended metaphor which in both instances suggests coldness, bleakness, and death. In the resolution of the poem, the speaker vows to join the lost baby in his watery death if she is ever less than a "mountain" to her "definite" children.

> if i am ever less than a mountain
> for your definite brothers and sisters
> let the rivers pour over my head
> let the sea take me for a spiller.[23]

The long untitled "the thirty-eight year" poem, is another example of a female blues lament. It depicts an ordinary woman—"plain as bread, round as cake"—attempting to reconcile the reality of her ordinary existence with her unfulfilled expectations.

> i had expected to be
> smaller than this,
> more beautiful,
> wiser in Afrikan ways
> more confident,
> i had expected
> more than this.[24]

In doubting her own accomplishments, the speaker begins to feel that she is destined to relive her mother's fate.

> my mother died at forty four
> a woman of sad countenance.[25]

Although she has become a mother herself and is

> surrounded by life,
> a perfect picture of
> blackness blessed,[26]

she is unable to free herself from the ghost of her mother's unfulfilled life.

This poem, like the traditional blues song, is a frank confrontation with self that bears no traces of self-pity or bitterness. It is a statement of the speaker's condition in an attempt to cope with its unflattering implications.

> i had expected more than this
> i had not expected to be
> an ordinary woman.[27]

A more diffuse view of Clifton's family is presented in *Generations*, a stylized family memoir, which uses Walt Whitman as a literary model to suggest celebration and self-discovery. It represents an ultimate attempt at reconciliation and synthesis of family, history, and the artist. Through the use of Whitmanesque cinematic cuts and cadences, *Generations* tells the story of the Sayles family in America.

The story is told to Clifton, in part, by her father, whose voice and presence dominate the book. Just as the Dahomey women are ideals of feminine strength and virtue, her father, Sam Sayles, is Clifton's ideal of masculine strength and fortitude. "He was a strong man, a rock,"[28] who is described in near-mythic proportions.

> He used to go to dances and sometimes in the
> middle of a dance he would get tired and throw
> his hat down and shout The Dance Is Over, and
> all the people would stop playing music and
> dancing and go home.[29]

In her poem "Daddy" written after his death, Clifton remembers him as

> . . . a confident man
> "I'll go to heaven," he said,
> "Jesus knows me."
> When his leg died, he cut it off.
> "It's gone," he said, "it's gone
> but I'm still here."[30]

Clifton's family in general and her father in particular are the stabilizing force upon which her work is drawn. Acknowledging suffering and simultaneously asserting the will to overcome it, as exemplified by her father, is a central tenet of her philosophy and a recurring theme in all of her work. This philosophy allows the poet to reconcile the dichotomy of personal/racial history—its mix of hopelessness and hope, of tragedy and triumph—with the realities of the present condition and to still feel fortunate. As Clifton's father once told her, "We fooled them, Lue, slavery was terrible but we fooled them old people. We came out of it better than they did."[31]

The optimism that permeates all of Clifton's work is fueled by her Christian faith. The tenets of Christianity are a natural vehicle for the espousal of her belief in the ultimate triumph and deliverance of an oppressed people. The biblical heroes and heroines that are cited in her poetry are examples of personal triumph over adversity, such as Daniel:

I have learned
some few things,
like when a man
walk manly
he don't stumble
even in the lion's den.[32]

These examples are analogues for modern man. We can overcome the temporary setbacks, like slavery; if in our minds we remain free, all is possible.

I rise above my self
like a fish flying

Men will be gods
if they want it.[33]

In the final analysis, the vindication that is promised the oppressed will come not only because it is just, and right and overdue—it will come because it is mandated by Divine Will.

While I was in the middle of the night
I saw red stars and black stars
pushed out of the sky by white ones
and I knew as sure as jungle
is the father of the world
I must slide down like a great dipper of stars
and lift men up.[34]

This, then, is the good news that Lucille Clifton tells. She dwells not on what Black people have been through but on the qualities that have enabled us to survive it all—and to keep right on.

NOTES

1. Lucille Clifton, *Good News About the Earth* (New York: Random House, 1972), editor's note.
2. Lucille Clifton, *Generations* (New York: Random House, 1976), p. 77.
3. Lucille Clifton, *Everett Anderson's Christmas Coming* (New York: Holt, Rinehart, 1971).
4. Lucille Clifton, *Some of the Days of Everett Anderson* (New York: Holt, Rinehart, 1970).
5. Lucille Clifton, *Everett Anderson's Year* (New York: Holt, Rinehart, 1971).
6. Lucille Clifton, *Good, Says Jerome* (New York: Dutton, 1973).

7. Lucille Clifton, *The Black BC's* (New York: Dutton, 1970).

8. Lucille Clifton, *An Ordinary Woman* (New York: Random House, 1974), p. 23.

9. Clifton, *Good News About the Earth*, p. 10.

10. Clifton, *Generations*, p. 78.

11. Clifton, *An Ordinary Woman*, p. 59.

12. Lucille Clifton, *Good Times* (New York: Vintage Books, 1970), p. 1.

13. Ibid., p. 38.

14. Ibid., p. 10.

15. Lucille Clifton, *An Ordinary Woman*, p. 19.

16. Clifton, *Good Times*, p. 19.

17. Clifton, *Generations*, p. 27.

18. Clifton, *An Ordinary Woman*, p. 73.

19. Ibid., p. 71.

20. Clifton, *Good Times*, p. 5.

21. Ibid., p. 18.

22. Clifton, *Good News About the Earth*, p. 4.

23. Ibid.

24. Clifton, *An Ordinary Woman*, p. 93.

25. Ibid.

26. Ibid.

27. Ibid.

28. Clifton, *Generations*, p. 24.

29. Ibid., p. 70.

30. Clifton, *Good News About the Earth*, p. 27.

31. Clifton, *Generations*, p. 58.

32. Lucille Clifton, *Good News About the Earth*, p. 35.

33. Ibid., p. 43.

34. Ibid., p. 44.

REFERENCES

Clifton, Lucille. The children's books and poetry books as cited.

Kent, George E. "The Poetry of Gwendolyn Brooks," *Black World* (September 1971).

Redmon, Eugene B. *Drumvoices: The Mission of Afro-American Poetry* (Garden City, NY: Anchor Press/Doubleday, 1976).

Watts, Emily Stipes. *The Poetry of American Women From 1632 to 1945* (University of Texas Press, Austin, TX 78712, 1978).

WILLIAM J. HARRIS

Sweet Soft Essence of Possibility: The Poetry of Nikki Giovanni

Even though Nikki Giovanni has a large popular audience, she has not gained the respect of the critics. Michele Wallace calls her "a kind of nationalistic Rod McKuen"; Eugene Redmond claims her poetry "lacks lyricism and imagery"; Haki Madhubuti (Don L. Lee) insists she lacks the sophistication of thought demanded of one with pretensions of a "political seer" and finally, Amiri Baraka and Saunders Redding, united on no other issue, declare in their different styles that she is simply an opportunist. These critics illustrate the problem of evaluating Nikki Giovanni dispassionately. Her limitations notwithstanding, there is a curious tendency of normally perceptive critics to undervalue her, to condescend to her rather than to criticize her.

When Michele Wallace compares Giovanni to McKuen, she is suggesting that both are popular poets. This is true enough, but still there is a crucial difference between them: McKuen is a bad popular poet; Giovanni is a good one. He is a bad popular poet because he presents conventional sentiments in a shamelessly sloppy form. His retellings of conventional stories in conventional ways, without a trace of thought or feeling, have won him a ready audience. In essence, he is the genius of the unexamined life; he is the opposite of a serious artist who is dedicated to the exploration of his life. The serious artist deals in fresh discoveries; McKuen in clichés. Giovanni, on the other

From *Black Women Writers (1950–1980)*, pp. 218–28. © 1984 by Mari Evans.

17

hand, is a popular poet but also a serious artist because she tries to examine her life honestly.

The popular writer is usually easy to read and topical; that is, he or she writes in a language which is direct and immediate rather than arcane or esoteric, and speaks of problems and situations that are obviously relevant to the general reader's life. This is neither good nor bad but simply the nature of the genre. Most critics, poets, and teachers are uncomfortable with the popular form. Since the language is unspecialized and the experience everyday, the critic and teacher are left virtually with very little to say, an embarrassing situation. Therefore, even the good popular poet is often ignored: one sees more essays on Wallace Stevens than on Langston Hughes. That the good popular poet is not analyzed is not the *poet's* fault; rather, current critical vocabularies and even values seem inadequate to deal with him. The good popular poet faces the complexity of life in his or her poems even though he does not embody it in their form. Langston Hughes may be one of America's greatest popular poets; he writes of celebrated subjects in a direct manner with the precision, toughness of language, and emotion which derive from the blues tradition. Conversely, McKuen's poetry derives from the tradition of pop song: at best the world of sentimentality, at worst the world of cynical lies. McKuen's carelessness of form, which can be found by randomly opening any of his books, testifies to his carelessness of thought and feeling. As Pound says: "Technique is the test of sincerity. If a thing isn't worth getting the technique to say, it is of inferior value."

Giovanni is a good popular poet: she is honest, she writes well-crafted poems, and, unlike McKuen, she pushes against the barriers of the conventional; in other words, she responds to the complexities of the contemporary world as a complex individual, not as a stock character in anybody's movie about Anyplace, U.S.A. In fact, much of Giovanni's value as a poet derives from her insistence on being herself; she refuses to go along with anybody's orthodoxy. Since she is always reacting to her multifarious environment, it is not surprising that her career has already gone through three distinct stages: first, the black militant; then the domestic lover; and now the disappointed lover. Therefore, it is clear that her move from Black militant poet to domestic woman poet is not a contradiction, as some critics maintain, but only a response to her times: the seventies and eighties call for different responses than did the sixties. Unlike Madhubuti she is not doctrinaire; she does not have a system to plug all her experiences into. She examines her time and place and comes to the conclusions she must for that time and place.

Giovanni does have weaknesses. At times she does not seem to think things through with sufficient care. Furthermore, she often does not bother to finish her poems; consequently, there are many unrealized poems in her oeuvre. Finally, not unlike a movie star, she is possibly too dependent on her public personality. In other words, she can be self-indulgent and irresponsible. Paradoxically, her shortcomings do grow out of the same soil as her strengths, that is, out of her independence of mind, her individuality, and her natural charm.

Since her first book in 1968, Nikki Giovanni has published a number of volumes of poetry, including *Black Feeling, Black Talk/Black Judgement* (a combined edition, 1970), *Re: Creation* (1970), *My House* (1972), *The Women and the Men* (1975), and her most recent work, *Cotton Candy on a Rainy Day* (1978), and even though her attitudes have changed over the years, the books are unified by her personality. Like many poets of the period she is autobiographical and her personal stamp is on all her work. There is also a consistency of style, even though there is a change of mood: the poetry is always direct, conversational, and grounded in the rhythms of Black music and speech. Her poems are also unified in that they are written from the perspective of a Black woman. Moreover, her themes remain constant: dreams, love, Blackness, womanhood, mothers, children, fathers, family, stardom, fame, and sex. In addition to her poetry books, she has published an autobiography, *Gemini*, two extended interviews—one with Margaret Walker, one with James Baldwin—and a number of children's books.

In Giovanni's first stage she wrote several classic sixties poems expressing the extreme militancy of the period. These include "The True Import of Present Dialogue, Black vs. Negro," and "For Saundra." In 1968 Giovanni spits out:

Nigger
Can you kill
Can you kill
Can a nigger kill
Can a nigger kill a honkie

The poem these lines are taken from, "The True Import of the Present Dialogue, Black vs. Negro," is intended to incite violence by asking for the literal death of white America. It captures the spirit of the sixties, that feeling that Armageddon, the final battle between good and evil, is imminent. It is informed by the example of Frantz Fanon, the Black revolutionary author of *The Wretched of the Earth*, whose book Eldridge Cleaver called "the Bible" of the Black liberation movement. In it, Fanon declares: "National liberation, national renaissance, the restoration of nationhood of the people, commonwealth: whatever may be the headings used or the new formulas introduced, decolonisation is always a violent phenomenon." Cleaver correctly claims that Fanon's book "legitimize[s] the revolutionary impulse to violence." No matter how romantic that moment now seems, there was then a sincere feeling that it was a time of revolution; and Giovanni, along with Madhubuti, Baraka and others, expressed these revolutionary ideas in their poems. Furthermore, Giovanni's poem "The True Import of Present Dialogue, Black vs. Negro" embodies more than the literal demand for the killing of whites: it also expresses a symbolic need on the part of Blacks to kill their own white values:

> Can you kill the nigger
> in you
> Can you make your nigger mind
> die

Eliot has said that poetry should not deviate too far from common speech; these Black revolutionary poets—in a sense Eliot's heirs—demonstrate that they have absorbed the subtleties of their language. For example, in the above poem Giovanni exploits the complex connotations of the term "nigger"; she uses it in this stanza to suggest the consciousness that wants to conform to white standards; consequently, to kill the "nigger" is to transform consciousness. In more general terms, the entire poem is cast in the form of a street chant: the rhythm is intended to drive the reader into the street, ready to fight. In fact, the source of much of the form utilized in the 1960s Black Arts Movement is street language and folk forms such as the chant and the dozens, a form of ritualized insult.

Giovanni's "For Saundra" provides the rationale for the New Black Poetry

> i wanted to write
> a poem
> that rhymes
> but revolution doesn't lend
> itself to be-bopping
>
> . . . . .
>
> maybe i shouldn't write
> at all
> but clean my gun

In short, Giovanni is saying that the times will not allow for poems which are not political in nature, which do not promote revolution. In the 1960s art had to subordinate itself to revolution. Ron Karenga insisted: "All art must reflect and support the Black Revolution."

Even though such revolutionary figures as Karenga and Baraka stressed collective over individual values, Giovanni remains an individual, implicitly questioning the call for revolutionary hatred in the very titles of such poems as "Letter to a Bourgeois Friend Whom Once I Loved (and Maybe Still Do If Love Is Valid)." She feels the tension between personal and revolutionary needs—a tension that runs throughout her work in the revolutionary period. Baraka demands: "Let there be no love poems written/until love can exist freely and cleanly." Giovanni understands that there are times of hate but also realizes that to subordinate all feeling to revolutionary hate is too abstract and inhuman.

Yet Giovanni's independence can be irresponsible. At times she seems a little too eager to gratify human desires at the expense of the revolution. She confides in "Detroit Conference of Unity and Art" (dedicated to former SNCC leader H. Rap Brown):

No doubt many important
Resolutions
Were passed
As we climbed Malcolm's ladder
But the most
Valid of them
All was that
Rap chose me

Even a nonrevolutionary reader would question the political commitment of the above lines. If one is going to set herself up as a serious poet-prophet— and Giovanni has—one had better be concerned about the revolutionary business at a meeting, not one's love life. This is the sort of frivolousness that Giovanni's critics, such as Madhubuti and Wallace, rightfully attack. However, at other times, Giovanni's frivolousness was refreshing in those tense and serious days of revolt. "Seduction" delightfully points out that the revolution cannot be conducted twenty-four hours a day. The poem centers around a brother so earnestly involved in the revolution that he does not notice that the poet has stripped both of them. The poem concludes:

then you'll notice
your state of undress
and knowing you you'll just say
"Nikki,
isn't this counterrevolutionary . . . ?"

Part of Giovanni's attractiveness stems from her realization that for sanity, there must be sex and humor, even in revolutionary times.

When the revolution failed her, Giovanni turned to love and began writing a more personal poetry, signaling the onset of the second stage of her career. The literature of the seventies was quite unlike those of the hot and hopeful sixties. Addison Gayle writes about certain important differences between the sixties and the seventies in his excellent autobiography, *Wayward Child*:

> Beyond my personal despair, there was that occasioned by the disappointments of the seventies, following so close upon the successes of the sixties, the return on almost all levels, to the old feelings of hopelessness, cynicism, and apathy, which, until the era of Martin King and Malcolm X, Stokely Carmichael, and H. Rap Brown, had so immobilized a race of people.

For Giovanni, too, idealism of the sixties had been replaced by the despair of the seventies. In a poem of the seventies she asserts:

> i've always prided myself
> on being a child of the sixties
> and we are all finished
> so that makes being
> nothing

The sixties stood for endless possibility; the seventies for hopelessness and frustration. However, in *My House* she seeks an alternative to public commitment and finds one in domestic love. Giovanni is not the only Black figure to seek new alternatives in the seventies: Cleaver found God; Baraka found Marxism; Julian Bond shifted allegiances from the activist organization SNCC to the staid NAACP. Giovanni finds her answers in "My House":

> i'm saying it's my house
> and i'll make fudge and call
> it love and touch my lips
> to the chocolate warmth
> and smile at old men and call
> it revolution cause what's real
> is really real
> and i still like men in tight

pants cause everybody has some
thing to give and more
important need something to take

and this is my house and you make me happy
so this is your poem

Giovanni has exchanged the role of revolutionary Mother Courage, sending
her Black troops into battle, for the role of domestic Black woman, making
fudge for her Black man. While the poem may make the reader uncomfortable—has it set the feminist movement back fifty years?—one can sympathize with Giovanni's desire to retreat into domestic comforts in the face of
a disappointing world. In "My House" she declares her domesticity loudly,
militantly, perhaps to give herself confidence in her new role. Later she will
celebrate the domestic more quietly and convincingly. In "Winter" from
Cotton Candy she observes:

Frogs burrow the mud
snails bury themselves
and I air my quilts
preparing for the cold
Dogs grow more hair
mothers make oatmeal
and little boys and girls
take Father John's Medicine
Bears store fat
chipmunks gather nuts
and I collect books
For the coming winter

Here Giovanni gathers supplies to retreat from the cold world; however, it
is only for a season. And unlike "My House," this poem creates a snug place
one would want to retire to; Giovanni has become more comfortably at
home in the domestic world of "Winter" than in the brash "My House."

If she implicitly questioned "pure" revolution earlier, in the seventies she
questions all ideologies that try to define or categorize her. In "Categories"
she writes:

and sometimes on rainy nights you see
an old white woman who maybe you'd really
   care about

except that you're a young Black woman
whose job it is to kill maim or seriously
make her question
the validity of her existence

. . . . . .

and if this seems
like somewhat of a tentative process it's probably
because I just realized that
I'm bored with categories

This suspicion of categories persists into *Cotton Candy*:

i am in a box
on a tight string
subject to pop
without notice

. . . . .

i am tired
of being boxed

. . . . .

i can't breathe

And we see in "A Poem Off Center" that Giovanni especially resents being
boxed in as a writer:

if you write a political poem
you're anti-semitic
if you write a domestic poem
you're foolish
if you write a happy poem
you're unserious
if you write a love poem
you're maudlin
of course the only real poem
to write

is the go to hell writing establishment poem
but the readers never know who

you're talking about which brings
us back
to point one

She has amusingly illustrated the dangers of literary categories. It is not surprising that this maverick does not want to be fenced in by anybody—friend or foe. She will not go along with anybody's orthodoxy.

By the third stage of her career, love, too, has failed Giovanni. In the title poem from her latest book, *Cotton Candy on a Rainy Day* (1978), she notes:

what this decade will be known for
There is no doubt it is loneliness

and in the same poem she continues:

If loneliness were a grape
  the wine would be vintage
If it were a wood
  The furniture would be mahogany
But since it is life it is
  Cotton Candy
    on a rainy day
The sweet soft essence
  of possibility
Never quite maturing

. . . . .

I am cotton candy on a rainy day
The unrealized dream of an idea unborn

Cotton Candy is Giovanni's bleakest book and reflects the failure of both revolution and love in the late seventies. Possibility has become stillborn.

Cotton Candy's bleak title poem provides a good example of the problems the reader faces in trying to evaluate Giovanni. Even though the poem is not a total success, it is better than it appears on casual reading. At first the title seems totally sentimental: "cotton candy" conjures up images of sticky, sappy love—it seems to catapult us into the world of Rod McKuen.

In fact, the publisher exploits this aspect of Giovanni's art by giving us a sentimental soft-pink cover featuring a drawing of a dreamy, romantic woman. It's a Rod McKuen cover. Despite the poem's sometimes vague language which suggests the conventional popular poem, "Cotton Candy" has serious moments which save it from the world of pop songs and greeting cards. When we look closely at the cotton candy image we see it refers to a world of failed possibility; and the language, at least for a few lines, is stately and expressive of a generation:

> The sweet soft essence of possibility
> Never quite maturing

A curious aspect of Giovanni's appeal has little to do with her language per se but with the sensibility she creates on the page. It isn't that she does not use words effectively. In fact, she does. Not only did she use Black forms effectively during the sixties; in the seventies she mastered a quieter, less ethnic, free verse mode. However, on the whole what is most striking about Giovanni's poetry is that she has created the charming persona of "Nikki Giovanni." This persona is honest, searching, complex, lusty, and, above all, individualistic and charmingly egoistical. This is a verbal achievement having less to do with the surface of language than with the creation of a character, that is, more a novelistic achievement than a lyric one.

Giovanni's lust is comedic (see "Seduction") and healthy; it permeates her vision of the world. Only a lusty woman would bring this perspective to the world of politics:

> Ever notice how it's only the ugly
> honkies
> who hate
> like hitler was an ugly dude
> same with lyndon

and only a lusty woman could write these joyful lines:

> i wanta say just gotta say something
> bout those beautiful beautiful beautiful outasight
> black men
> with they afros
> walking down the street
> is the same ol danger
> but a brand new pleasure

A source of her unabashed lustiness could be the tough, blues-woman tradition. She could be following in the footsteps of Aretha Franklin's "Dr. Feelgood." The following Giovanni poem explicitly exploits and updates the blues/soul tradition:

> its wednesday night baby
> and i'm all alone
> wednesday night baby
> and i'm all alone
>
> . . . . .
>
> but i'm a modern woman baby
> ain't gonna let this get me down
>
> i'm a modern woman
> ain't gonna let this get me down
> gonna take my master charge
> and get everything in town

This poem combines the classic blues attitude about love—defiance in the face of loss—with references to contemporary antidotes to pain: charge cards.

The poem "Ego Tripping," one of her best poems, grounded in the vital Black vernacular, features her delightful egotism. The poem is a toast, a Black form where the hero establishes his virtues by boasting about them. Her wonderfully healthy egotism, which is expressed succinctly in these witty lines: "show me some one not full of herself/and i'll show you a hungry person" abounds in "Ego Tripping":

> I was born in the congo
> I walked in the fertile crescent and built
>   the sphinx
> I designed a pyramid so tough that a star
>   that only glows every one hundred years falls
>   into the center giving divine perfect light
> I am bad

In a way "Ego Tripping" is an updating of Hughes' "The Negro Speaks of Rivers" from a woman's perspective. Hughes' poem is a celebration of the collective Black experience from the primordial time to the present. Giovanni's poem creates a giant mythic Black woman who embodies and celebrates the race across time. The poem doesn't only claim that Giovanni is Black and proud: it creates a magnificent Black woman whose mere gaze can burn out a Sahara Desert and whose casual blowing of her nose can provide oil for the entire Arab world. In a word, she is "bad!" Since it is not Giovanni speaking personally but collectively, it is not a personal boast but a racial jubilee.

Giovanni is a frustrating poet. I can sympathize with her detractors, no matter what the motives for their discontent. She clearly has talent that she refuses to discipline. She just doesn't seem to try hard enough. In "Habits" she coyly declares:

> I sit writing
> a poem
> about my habits
> which while it's not
> a great poem
> is mine

It isn't enough that the poem is hers; personality isn't enough, isn't a substitute for fully realized poems. Even though she has created a compelling persona on the page, she has been too dependent on it. Her ego has backfired. She has written a number of lively, sometimes humorous, sometimes tragic, often perceptive poems about the contemporary world. The best poems in her three strongest books, *Black Feeling, Black Talk/Black Judgement, Re: Creation,* and *Cotton Candy*, demonstrate that she can be a very good poet. However, her work also contains dross: too much unrealized abstraction (flabby abstraction at that!), too much "poetic" fantasy posing as poetry and too many moments verging on sentimentality. In the early seventies, after severely criticizing Giovanni's shortcomings, Haki Madhubuti said he eagerly awaited the publication of her new book, *Re: Creation*; he hoped that in it she would fulfill the promise of her early poetry. Even though it turned out to be one of Giovanni's better books, I find myself in a similar situation to Madhubuti's. I see that not only does Giovanni have promise, she already has written some good poems and continues to write them. Yet I am concerned about her development. I think it is time for her to stand back and take stock of herself, to take for herself the time for reflection, the vacation she says Aretha deserves for work well done. Nikki Giovanni is one of the most talented writers to come out of the Black sixties, and I don't want to lose her. I want her to write poems which grow out of that charming persona, not poems which are consumed by it. Giovanni must keep her charm and overcome her self-indulgence. She has the talent to create good, perhaps important, poetry, if only she has the will to discipline her craft.

MAX W. THOMAS

Carl Phillips and Reginald Shepherd
Mighty Lines

> But know you not that creatures wanting sense
> By nature have a mutual appetence,
> And wanting organs to advance a step,
> Moved by love's force, unto each other leap?
> Much more in subjects having intellect
> Some hidden influence breeds like effect.
>
> —Christopher Marlowe, *Hero and Leander*

Mutual appetence, intelligence, hidden influence: perhaps Marlowe has been waiting all this time for some pastoral heirs. But it's not just subject matter or diction in Phillips' *Pastoral* and Shepherd's *Wrong* that make me think of Marlowe. Instead it's the fact that they follow the less obvious, and rarely followed, footsteps of erotic redefinition that Marlowe left behind.

I find it hard to imagine why, with those gorgeous translations of the *Amores* and the true perversity of *Hero and Leander*, Marlowe is remembered primarily as the author of a catchy little ditty, rather than as a subtle theorist of desire. Sure, Marlowe writes about passion, and sex, notoriously—indeed, Marlowe is often discussed as the queer poet *ne plus ultra* of the Renaissance. His queerness, I would submit, is not an element of any homoeroticism in the texts, however: after all, male desire for men, particularly boys, is an entirely *normal* state of affairs in Renaissance pastoral poetry, as in the Roman models

From *The Iowa Review*, vol. 30, no. 2 (Fall, 2000): pp. 169–75. Copyright © 2000 by *The Iowa Review*.

29

from which it draws. Marlowe's queerness, rather, lies in his subversion of still-current models of pleasure and desire which emphasize either the economic connotations of seed-spending or the Petrarchan model of desire as a function of lack. Marlowe's model of desire is of the infinite brink: Hero and Leander keep thinking they've exhausted themselves only to find even more pleasant things to do to each other; even Neptune finds pleasure, rather than Petrarchan woe, in Leander's unattainability.

Phillips and Shepherd both write about sex too, beautifully, perversely, arousingly, lyrically, bluntly, frequently. That's part of the genius of Phillips' title and collection: he writes a poetry in which sex between men is the ordinary, even classical, state of affairs, one in which it is entirely more remarkable to think about a stag in the woods than an erection. And both of them announce themselves in their titles as mounting a full-frontal embrace of that which is denigrated. Phillips quotes from *Lamentations* "Let him put his mouth in the dust—there may yet be hope"; Shepherd from Beckett (our modern master of lamentation): "All I know is what words know, and the dead things … Wrong, very rightly wrong," making certain that we get both the sense of abjection and the sense of liberation that accompanies the mouthing of dust, dead things, words.

They share with Marlowe an attraction to the abject, and an impulse to transvalue abject desire, yes. But even more crucially, they share with Marlowe a recognition that such transvaluation is a matter of form and genre, of *poetics* in the largest sense, even more than of sexual acts. Where inexpert hands and mouths proffer an uncritical preference for the underbelly, the results mostly make "us"—fellow travelers and staid normals alike—cringe at self-revelation of unpleasant habits. The potential in pastoral is to take the "simple" swain's song, make it melodious, and yet also give it an edge. The best Elizabethan straight pastoral (Sidney, Drayton) manages to critique even as it warbles in hendecasyllables. And the best Elizabethan queer pastoral is of course Marlowe's, where the shepherds and sheep are not just under-ground but under water, literally in the mouth of Neptune, in those famously mighty pentameter lines.

Both Shepherd and Phillips, I think, succeed, in such a direction, for what they attend to is not a particular sexual practice, but rather the very poetics that gives that practice meaningful shape. They accomplish a nuancing not just of attention but of lineation and lineage, too: they bear with them the richness, and some of the troubled perversity, of work that carries itself so well as to resist critique, and so risks instead appearing immaculate, even as its concerns are as maculate, and as hard, as it gets. That, of course, is the problem of pastoral. Its often self-deprecating amorousness ("it's only love, after all") yokes together *sprezzatura* (a virtuoso denial of virtuosity) with earnestness ("it's love, after all"), and dares you to see its polished surface as the thing itself.

Desire An Sich

The thing itself, in both of these books, is part of the stake: where it is located, how we apprehend it. For Shepherd, an encounter, any encounter perhaps, is made visible at the expense of certain knowledge. Time and light may be the metiers of the encounter, but they are stand-ins; each destination is not the place but an inclination:

> The soul absents itself into a stranger's
> several bodies, distracted
> by opacity, each man a destination
> to other men. The width of a moment
>
> contains them, sustains them at the site
> of sight, the charm of unmotivated appearance
> in his first meetings with light.
> ("This History of His Body")

Or, in a beautiful twisting together of revenge fantasy (you'll-be-sorry-when-I'm-gone) and sexual fantasy (no-one-will-ever-love-you-like-I-do), "Also Love You" imagines the true element of love to be in the future. "I think of you when I am dead, the way rocks / think of earthworms," the poem begins, and proceeds to catalogue a hyper-anthropomorphic fidelity of the earth and everything on it: "I'll be the things / left behind for you, I'll be much kinder / then." The speaker here alternates between "will" as a measure of his state to come and as a trope of the legacy he leaves to the beloved, but what remains in flux between those senses of the word is the very *thing* that constitutes Eros: whether it is tangibly a feature of desire, or something proffered to the object of desire.

In the process here, and in many poems, Shepherd revisits a model of desire as lack, suggesting that the question may not be one of lack or plenitude, but of leaving a mark on the object of your desire. In a witty reformulation of Anne Carson's reformulation of Sappho's *glukopikron* (sweetbitter), "Eros is bitter, and bitterly proud" ("About a Boy"). Eros, cupid-like, seems to hover somewhere behind the encounter, impelling it but not *of it*. "Poor Eros. His arms are broken off / at the shoulder, his eyes have worn / shut." So too, the observer/desirer in these poems has a curious relation to his desire: feeling it, but not quite generating it. Men appear and disappear; the sun appears and disappears; snow changes; "blue meets blue . . . sky / meets the sky": encounters all, but particularly in the first three of the four sections of the book, the events seem to occur without regard for the observer, the desirer, the body marked by them.

Phillips, too, models desire, and not through lack. Here, it's more a matter of repetition, as in "The Fountain":

Crests.
And Falls.
    We're here, again.
        We're
at the beach.
    You're where you've
been, the water.

You leave the water.

The water leaves your body like what knows
it can afford to, at last.

Individual words and sounds establish, through both audible and conceptual rhyming, a quasi-sexual pulse, followed by something like satiation, but not satiation itself: "Routinely the sea, / unbuckling, out- / swells the frame it will // return to, be / held restively / by" ("All Art . . ."). Only in this landscape does the sea, normally so contained in its bed, go cruising, unbuckling itself. So often an image of what-is-longed-for, here the sea itself longs, not to be filled but to overflow. Even the motif of post-mortem desire cannot be still, but still hungers: "his body was // his body, already bringing me / gifts from a dead world: that last morning / . . . / . . . So many relics, / without the power of // so many relics" ("Portage"). Or, later in the same poem, doves ("unswallowable," not the tuneful birds of lyric but the peaceable reminders of the lamentations now over but not unfelt), metonymize the problem of repetition and identity "once, twice," "visibly // themselves," "forever stuck inside / their excellent, downed throats." Series, tautology, geometric impossibility (that down stays up in the throat; that down migrates from outside to inside) serve to figure forth desire as a kind of polyvalent reliquary, something that achieves its force by virtue of revisitation. The thing itself is not found, not encountered, not sustained: it seems to be that which interposes itself, for both of these poets, in the moment of apprehension and experiential vertigo.

Elemental Might

There's a lot of weather in these poems. Plenty of seas and seasons; of meadows, lakes, vistas; of places. Woods and the woods' shadows. Dusks, moons. Phillips, in particular, produces pastoral settings for nearly philosophical poems: there are even occasional deer (although the old puns on hart/heart, chased/chaste, are left largely latent). This is only to be expected of a book entitled *Pastoral*, of course, but "it's desire again, passing / us by, souveniring us with / gospel the grass turned / choir, leans into" ("The Truth"). Even the line breaks suggest how fraught this field is, how now that the shouting is all over there is only the barely audible grass to hearken toward. Like the crepuscular and chiaroscuric places in these poems, the nearly mute pastoral does not yield itself up to allegory easily, resists shouting. Moreover, in "Retreat":

> Come spring, then summer, the boats
>
> that come instead will be for finding
> pleasure because, simply, it's findable
> here, and still free, even if, just now,
>
> who will say so? Nobody's here.

It's the appeal of the forgotten place, the meadow out of season, that lets attention *attune* the mind and the body, throughout *Pastoral*.

Wrong takes a different, similarly subtle, nearly alchemical tack. Plotted or not, there's a nearly elemental progression through the sections of the book: Water, Wind, Earth, respectively, become the leitmotifs for parts 1, 2, and 3. Sometimes their forms are distorted (blood for water, kiss for air, maps for earth), and no section is without the others (water and maps, particularly, pervade the book) but the atomism is detectable, even flaunted—"I've been asked to write about vampires, / so I will write of the lake and its three winds: gust, gale, and blast" ("Vampires"). Elsewhere, it's a faint pattern, and one that, fortunately, doesn't dominate any single poem or section, but rather one that whispers, as does Phillips' grass, that there's something primordial lurking here.

> They lose their sainthood there
> to birds they hear of, then
> they hear: the mutilated stories of gods, branches
> broken off or left unfinished, attributes
>
> sheared off to sheer description, reasons
> slurred to wind-surge blurring leaves.
> All power and no substance, hardened
> into profile and other approximations

of a man. The world has resisted thought
so long, the youth of trees concealed.
    ("The History of His Body")

The world is the world, but it bears in it the forces of the elements and the traces of gods. Only by looking aslant, by looking "wrong," by transvaluing the almost archaic qualities of poetry's Orphic mysteries, does the full texture of these poems, Phillips' and Shepherds' both, fully shine. That is why literal accounts of the events of these poems seem to me to be beside the point: the poems stick to event just enough to point toward this alchemical shadow world, where correspondence matters almost more than objecthood, where signs are not symbols but spurs:

  The gods are far,
we're told. Maybe. I do not
call the gods gone, nor
call it force, for—I swayed
easy, as

  will a field,
unto fire. . . .
    ("And Fitful Memories of Pan," part IV, "Dropped Flute")

Fire, of course, is the missing element above. And it's missing, at least in its blatant form, in these poems, too. What is there instead is *light*: "lucid // distortion" (Shepherd, "Motive"), "invisible // curves on the air / to mark what was let go" (Phillips, "Unbeautiful"). In several tremendous poems of light, particularly Shepherd's "Kneeling Self Portrait," and "Brightens," and in Phillips' "Study, Between Colors" and "Animal," there is a constant and persistent attention to the ways that light is both a source of radiation and something reflected, that which makes sight, and insight, possible, both in the moments of its brightness and in its dusk. Shepherd refers to "a prism / or this unrequited reticence" ("Lens"), and this paradoxical quality of exposing all without any self-disclosure is what seems to constitute the motive force turning the world that the desiring speakers in these poems inhabit. In the conditional, not the muscular, sense, these are *might-y* lines.

Lines

Although I've discussed them in rather close quarters, and although they share similar concerns, the poems are unmistakable. Phillips moves toward a sparser and sparser line, and a cascade of repeated phrases, words, and sounds, often with attenuated grammar: "Less the shadow / than you a stag, sudden, through it. // Less the stag breaking cover than // the antlers, with which/crowned" ("Hymn"), often with layered consciousnesses: "*let me. / As snow upon, / into any vale, / that vale—// we have been/places, times—/* where has always lain/historically // temptation . . ." ("Lay Me Down"). These short lines have an unerring sense of the line break, using syntax against sense against breath to build undisclosed connections. Such breaks stitch together what might otherwise be stock devices of "hesitation" or "fragmentation."

Shepherd, on the other hand, prefers a more traditionally phrasal line, and the rhythm of thought, as of sub-vocalization, in these poems is achieved in longer units: the stanza or the strophe, rather than the line-break. Not strictly metered, the lines nevertheless often bear about the duration of a pentameter line. In "Some Maps," Shepherd turns accentual on us, approximating the alliteration, caesura, and double-beat half-lines of Anglo-Saxon prosody and diction ("A scree heaped on the steep of it / Was rubble, ruin, rubbish-heap and history / The underneath unearthed.") Where Phillips seems to seek a line attuned to a mode of thought, Shepherd seems to be plumbing the possibilities of an inherited line, "to open these locked doors of language" ("Crepuscular").

The Pastoral Condition

Phillips and Shepherd, despite their differences in strategy, in mode, and in effect, seek out a model of desire which neither celebrates the transgressive uncritically nor subsumes it to dominant paradigms, which is serious without being earnest. Earnestness is no longer really poetry's long suit, if it ever was. Yet earnestness is just what these poems remind us we clamor for. We want our icing, and our cake too, and we don't want either to be good for us. In the process, they begin a reinvention of that queerest of literary forms, the pastoral Eclogue. Perhaps we're ready for pastoral again.

ELIZABETH DODD

The Great Rainbowed Swamp: History as Moral Ecology in the Poetry of Michael S. Harper

Profit, Pleasure, and Ecocriticism

I want to consider the absence of black writers from existing ecocritical discussion. Leonard Lutwack says flatly, "American wilderness writing ignores the black, because of his association with agriculture" (72). I suspect that African American writers may not have embraced nature writing (creative writing in the autobiographical naturalist tradition) since what Robinson Jeffers called Inhumanism (the literary attempt to deflect attention away from human beings, or what Glen A. Love calls ego-consciousness) might not be appealing for writers who already feel politically, economically, and socially marginalized. Further, academic inquiry, including the work of ecocritics, already expects black literature to focus on the social realm; literary studies categorizes black literature as offering an interest in environment similar to the interest in socioeconomic environment that characterized naturalist novels at the close of the nineteenth century.

As ecocritics articulate the complex and often conflicted attitudes toward the North American continent that contribute to a sense of place, we should not overlook black writing whose obvious focus is sociopolitical. An examination of the underlying attitudes toward nature that are encoded in literary works can contribute to what Neil Evernden calls "what it feels like to have a territory" (97)—or what it feels like not to. As Lutwack notes, "[human] use of the earth's resources, [our] alteration of places in every corner of the globe,

---

must proceed now with a view not only to present profit and pleasure but to the survival of the very next generation" (2). African American writers who focus on this continent's long relationship with slavery have a unique perspective on both profit and pleasure, and an examination of their work from an ecocritical perspective can illuminate previously unrecognized aspects of the work, increasing our understanding of how sense of place and ethical awareness intersect.

In the poetry of Michael S. Harper, race and gender are clearly primary interests. Born in Brooklyn in 1938, Harper began a rapid sequence of publishing in 1970, with six collections appearing by 1975. Selections from these books appear with groups of newer poems in *Images of Kin: New and Selected Poems* (1977). An early poem entitled "Brother John" begins:

> Black man:
> I'm a black man;
> I'm black; I am—
> A black man; black—
>   (1–4)

Yet Harper's interests are wider than might be supposed. As an editor once said dismissively of Norman MacLean's stories (qtd. in Love 255), Harper's later poems "have trees in them." Living in the New England countryside, in a house dating to the early nineteenth century, Harper sees that each tree holds in its woody tissue the literal and figurative bones of history. Place—the material world of a particular locale—is infused with the ethical consequences of historical actions. In Harper's eye, landscape becomes history, history becomes landscape, and the ecocritic can find in this intermingling some important challenges to the destinies that Western imperialists once declared manifest. Harper unpeels the layers of social history involved in the American view of land as commodity. His work offers a rich nexus for environmental history and ecocriticism as well as social history and the enduring value of modernist poetic technique.

History as Moral Ecology

Harper was a relative newcomer to Rhode Island when he joined the faculty at Brown University in 1971, having moved from Brooklyn as a teenager to southern California. He attended high school and college in Los Angeles, earned an M.F.A. at the Writers' Workshop at the University of Iowa in 1963, and held a number of short-term positions at schools along the Pacific coast before moving to Barrington, Rhode Island. Harper soon turned his work toward the study of New England history while he explored the fields and cemeteries surrounding his new home. Learning the untold aspects of colonial history as well as those more familiar is a way to root himself in his new home place, a form of what Gary Snyder calls "reinhabitation: moving back into a terrain that has been abused and half-forgotten" (178). Michael Harper has said, "with luck we are learning animals, but we are in the ecology, and probably falsely at the 'deified' godhead of the triangle; without a certain ruthless ingenuity our wreckage might have been less."[1]

We see this reinhabitation enacted vividly in Harper's poem "History as Apple Tree," which appeared in *Song: I Want a Witness* in 1972. The larger poem sequence focuses on the locale of Dighton, Massachusetts, and constitutes a part of Harper's ruminations on—and rootings into—New England. For three dense and highly allusive stanzas, he recounts details from early Puritan settlement of the colony, but he claims connection not with Massachusetts Colony's John Winthrop and Rhode Island Colony founder Roger Williams, nor with the early settler and trader Richard Smith, but instead with the indigenous Narragansetts and their chief sachem, Canonicus. As Harper notes, African slaves sometimes found freedom in the wilderness by escaping their European masters and joining native communities, a fact more widely recognized among the Seminoles of Florida (whom Harper mentions elsewhere).[2] Harper implies the bitterly ironic contrast to the greater religious freedom enjoyed in the early colony (compared with the Puritan stronghold of Massachusetts), for Rhode Island had a slave population in colonial times. Indeed, at his death in 1692, Richard Smith left a sizeable estate, including eight African slaves (Bailyn 99). By 1708, the colony levied a tax on slave importation as a source of revenue; from roughly 1725 until 1807, a period when commerce far exceeded agriculture in the economy, Rhode Island relied heavily on slave trading. One historian explains that Rhode Island was the only colony where the slave trade "assume[d] long-term social and economic significance" to the extent that it "was the principal American carrier" (Coughtry 5–6).

Further, Harper complicates reader expectations of a polarized racial relationship. Rather than a clear tension of whites versus people of color, Rhode Island's history contains another irony. While Williams's banishment from Massachusetts Colony in 1635 followed from his religious differences with the Puritan establishment, he also protested the method of land acquisition through royal charter, which ignored Native American land rights altogether. Williams's published criticisms (which do not survive) incurred the protestations of both John Winthrop and John Cotton, who each voiced a version of the Anglo immigrants' attitudes. Winthrop claimed that land lying "common, and hath never been replenished or subdued is free to any that possess or improve it"; Cotton wrote derisively of Native American land use,

"We did not conceive that it is a just title to so vast a continent, to make no other improvement of millions of acres in it, but only to burn it up for pastime" (qtd. in Gaustad 32). In contrast, Williams maintained a close relationship with the Narragansett sachems Canonicus and Miantonomi, learning their language and publishing *A Key into the Language of America*, a dictionary focusing significantly on the words and phrases needed to establish Anglo-Native American trade. In 1962 Perry Miller declared, "Williams could treat Indian culture with respect. He was the only Englishman in his generation who could do so" (52).

While Harper's poem introduces these historical details, he claims that knowledge requires physical contact as well as abstract comprehension. This is the kind of assertion already familiar to ecocritics and wilderness writers. Harper recounts a legend of how a huge apple tree grew over Roger Williams's grave until two centuries later

> dust and root grew
> in his human skeleton:
> bones became apple tree.
>   (37–39)

Harper then describes his need to touch both place and past in order to take hold of his own presence and belonging.

> As black man I steal away
> in the night to the apple tree,
> place my arm in the rich grave . . .
> take up a chunk of apple root,
> let it become my skeleton . . .
> my arm the historical branch,
> my name the bruised fruit . . .
>   (40–42, 44–45, 47–48)

The poem's title, "History as Apple Tree," suggests that history can become as matter; the living presence of a tree holds the body of the past in its tissue, while by taking root, Harper allows both the place and its past inhabitants to live in him. Yes, this is a symbolic family tree, but it is very much a real tree, more akin to Robert Frost's apple or beech trees than to William Faulkner's metaphoric family trees of white patrimony, for example. Further, it calls to mind Toni Morrison's notion that, beyond the mind's capacity to recall events and their locations, "rememory" means that, as the ex-slave Sethe explains in *Beloved*, "Places, places are still there. . . . What I remember is a picture floating around out there outside my head. I mean, even if I don't think about it, even if I die, the picture of what I did, or knew, or saw is still out there. Right in the place where it happened" (36). Actions become embodied in the landscape, surviving their actors and remaining in their original location. Morrison, as do Harper and Faulkner, emphasizes the physical durability of moral consequences, in opposition to the notion common in contemporary white society that the damaging injustices of centuries of slavery should no longer play a tangible role in contemporary black-white relations or in black social structures.

Most significant to the ecocritic are the formal and thematic surprises this poem holds. Purporting to be condensed narrative, an historical account, "History as Apple Tree" abruptly abandons narrative for metaphoric epiphany. This is not an Emersonian transcendental epiphany; instead, its epiphany descends to the ground beneath one's feet. Simultaneously, while appearing to consider social and political questions of race in America—Native American, African, and European—the poem subtly suggests that social history has an inescapable effect on physical environment. Thus racism becomes not only a cultural legacy that gets handed on but, through its connections to trade and both Roger Williams's and Richard Smith's early Rhode Island settlements in the form of trading posts, it becomes part of the land, with an ecological legacy that envelops the culture that follows.[3] In the context Harper surveys, the religious struggle that prompted early white Rhode Islanders to leave Massachusetts takes on socioeconomic importance as well, resonating in the poem's intriguing line *"How does patent not breed heresy?"* (5, emphasis in original).

Uplift from a Dark Tower

The significance of mercantilist and capitalist trade, which find their logical extreme in the commodification of people—what Harper elsewhere calls, in a chillingly layered allusion, "sex fingers toes / in the marketplace" (*Images of Kin* "Dear John, Dear Coltrane" 1–2)—is further explored in a series of four poems titled collectively "Uplift from a Dark Tower" and included in *Images of Kin: New and Selected Poems*. I want to supply detailed close reading of a few individual poems and then return to consider the poems' contribution toward a more fully American ecocriticism. Harper's exploration of what W. E. B. Du Bois called "the problem of the color line" (xxiii) has important implications for our urgently needed development of an environmental ethic. While Harper's title *Images of Kin* emphasizes human interconnectedness, the quiet role of place in the "Uplift" series extends beyond questions of transracial and transgenerational kinship. In Harper's moral ecology, thoughtful examination of social history entails attention to the treatment of both persons and places. His interest is similar to that of Annette Kolodny, when she argues that the marriage of Pocahontas to John Rolfe was "a kind of objective correlative for the possibility of the Europeans' actually possessing the charms inherent in the virgin continent" (5). As Kolodny makes clear, the personification of place ("virgin continent") and the objectification of persons (especially in this case, Native American women) are closely connected in the myth of American settlement.

Harper's "Uplift" poems make clear reference to the fact that he composed them during his stay at Yaddo, the well-known writers' colony in Saratoga Springs, New York. During his use of the tower studio in the mansion-style, nineteenth-century house, Harper is an indirect beneficiary of Spencer Trask and Katrina (Kate Nichols) Trask, a wealthy couple who purchased the estate in 1881 and eventually set up a trust to establish the colony. As Katrina Trask described her vision for the estate to her husband, "Yaddo is not to be an institution, a school, a charity: it is to be, always, a place of inspiration, a delightful, hospitable home where guests may come and find welcome.... At Yaddo they will find the inspiration they need.... Look, Spencer, they are walking in the woods, wandering in the garden, sitting under the pine trees—men and women—creating, creating, creating!" (193).

The exhilarated tone seems indicative of Katrina Trask's enthusiastic and romantic sense of life; it is decidedly in contrast to the fact-packed syntax in Harper's poems. The Trasks were eccentric idealists, dedicating their home at Yaddo to the pursuit of their notion of chivalry, full of medieval pageantry and literary allusion. Although the majority of Katrina Trask's memoir, *Yaddo: The Story of Yaddo*, details parties, masques, and other social events of her time as "Katrina Regina, Queen of Yaddo," Harper finds it to be one of several sources that inform the poems he writes during his stay in the tower, originally Katrina Trask's library-study.

The layering of geography with history, people with place, and economy with ecology takes its most developed form in the last poem of the series, "Psychophotos of Hampton." Earlier poems in the "Uplift" series have contemplated Booker T. Washington's problematic belief in economic uplift for African Americans through industrial education at his Tuskegee Institute—which, incidentally, received funding from philanthropists such as George Foster Peabody, a close friend of Spencer Trask and Katrina Trask (and Katrina's second husband after Spencer's death). Here Harper goes further back, to Washington's education at Hampton Institute in Virginia.

The layering takes form in stanza-long sentences, piling clause against clause without clear grammatical connectives. In the fourteen-line opening stanza, Harper takes us halfway across the continent, from Yaddo's comfortable room and board and across the Adirondacks to Canada—where

"French/Indian alliances" are based on the currency of beaver pelts (8). We then cross the western plains, where the buffalo were slaughtered, and on to Utah, where "runaway bigamists" settle at the Great Salt Lake (11). By now the page is littered with corpses, from beavers trapped for the European pelt market to bison shot for hides, tongues, or in pursuit of extermination of the Plains Indians, whose culture depended on the great herds.

I find this a dizzying journey, especially since it is made not only in the company of Harper but also Etienne, an African who served in the Trask household in 1881. Trask, whom Harper briefly quotes, mentions Etienne in her *Story of Yaddo*, speaking of having tutored him prior to his training for "missionary service" and describing how he doubled as her "guardian and protector" since she had no other "man-servant."

> One night after midnight, I opened my door, thinking I heard a noise downstairs: there, just outside the threshold, lay Etienne, a most startling sight. He was the blackest black man that could be imagined: he lay on his back, stretched to his full length, sound asleep, and in his hand was a large carving knife! The fear that had impelled me to open the door was as nothing compared to my sudden fear of Etienne, the son of a cannibal, a carving knife in his hand, at my door! It was true no one could pass him to come to me—but it was also true I could not pass him to escape, if his hereditary tendencies should assert themselves.... Etienne's pride lay in the pure strain of his cannibal ancestry. His mind was quick and altogether unexpected: he learned very fast and had most amazing opinions about life. Once, when I was talking with him of the African race, he said a very true thing: he said it was merely a question of the sun on his outside—"My body may be black, but my soul is white." Candour compels me to confess that, after having sharpened his wits at our American institutions, his missionary zeal failed to develop, and he went back to Africa as—a trader! (Trask 78–79)

While no more than three pages of the 214-page monograph address Trask's "long interest" in "the colored race," these few paragraphs contribute significantly to Harper's history of Yaddo. It is a history filled with ironies, which Harper presents without explanation. However, Harper has clearly intended readers to find contexts: he even notes that the Trask memoir is privately printed, as if to help in our interlibrary loan searches (*Images of Kin* 27).[4]

The "having sharpened his wits" and "cannibal ancestry" from Trask's prose are syntactically fused in Harper's "Psychophotos of Hampton," becoming "his cannibal ancestry sharpened by" the combination of landscape and history that follows in lines 7–14. Not only did Etienne learn quickly, Harper implies, he learned thoroughly from the Trasks, whose fortune came from Spencer's skill as an investment banker. Despite his missionary-sponsor's intentions, Etienne learns that the true lesson America teaches is capitalism, where anything can be converted to commodity. Booker T. Washington also learned this lesson, Harper suggests; the poem begins with an epigraph noting that Washington owed his career to the white founder of Hampton Institute, General Samuel Chapman Armstrong, with whose enthusiasm he launched the project of Tuskegee—uplift through industrial education.

Education continues as a theme for the poems, as "Psychophotos" focuses more closely on Hampton Institute. Although the institute began under the auspices of the Freedman's Bureau for former slaves (the first classes are said to have been held under a great oak, the Emancipation Tree), the United States pursued its long policy of assimilation of Native Americans here as well. In Harper's words, "At $68/head, the great Dakotah nation went to college"—line 28 opens with the language of commodity, so many dollars per unit. As Harper "walk[s] out over swampgrounds, campsites" (33), the poem turns toward elegy or memorial, listing sixteen names of the dead, "their souls finally saved / from the highlands where they were born" (74–75). These are young people, ranging in age from infancy to twenty-two—most are in their teens. Nearly all are Sioux, from the Dakotas; two are from Arizona pueblos; and one is from South Africa.

We have thus returned to a mingling of nations of color, red and black, treated in the earlier "History as Apple Tree." In the next stanza of "Psychophotos," Harper moves beyond the specific extinctions of spirit listed among the dead young people. We find "the common man of Andrew / Jackson" (99–100) seeking in the wars of 1816–1818 to exterminate the Seminole nation in Florida, largely because the tribe had a significant black population living in a freedom that would, by its proximity to southern plantations, weaken the institution of U.S. slavery.

After these glimpses at assimilation and extermination as major U.S. policies toward nonwhites, Harper turns to the nineteenth-century novelist Herman Melville and his "scrimshaw tales" (126). Scrimshaw is an art form carved on the bones from the bodies of whales slaughtered for oil production; originally a leisure pastime for whaling sailors, it derives directly from capitalist slaughter. Harper implies that the paradigm has a close similarity to the way "the Renaissance [was] built on slave trading" (137). It also parallels Katrina Trask's buoyant but ironic wish for artists to engage in leisured, elegant creating on the grounds of her estate. For, in another poem of Harper's "Uplift" series, "Dining from a Treed Condition, An Historical

Survey," we learn that the first white owner of the land was Jacobus Barhyte, a Revolutionary War officer who was an "American patriot" (33); he was also a slaveholder. The ease and luxury Trask described will rest atop the labor—and so the bodies—of those eighteenth-century slaves who worked the land.

By now the poem's journey is nearly over, and Harper stands at "the terrace overhang" for a "last view" (132–33). The vista is, of course, the handsome gardens and grounds of the Yaddo estate; yet this created order and beauty do not have the last say. Instead, the poem turns deliberately away from the mood Trask had hoped for artists in her beloved tower. In her memoir she wrote of her delight there: "My high Tower was a consummation! O room of rooms, where my mountains and the spurs of three other ranges may be seen; the glorious colours of the sunrise flush it at Dawn, and at Even the vivid splendour of the sunset. To this Tower the chosen came [but] ... [a]lthough the Tower is a shrine to friendship, it is also a room for work" (27). Later she describes the view the room affords her: "The great eastern window in the Tower commands the thirty miles of rolling valley, and the wondrous range of mountains from whence my help [hired servants] has come through all these changing years" (154).

Harper articulates a different mood and view both of and from the tower. The time frame is unspecific, and, toothbrush in hand (in a playful gesture toward Booker T. Washington's insistence on hygiene, especially the brushing of teeth), Harper observes:

> the talk was of politics,
> rhetoric, and the literature of the great
> rainbowed swamp from the vision of the black tower.
>   (143–45)

This could be a conversation among writers at the colony during his stay, but it carries a layered sense of the nineteenth-century Trask dinner table as well. Trask titled one chapter "Table Talk at Yaddo," and she makes clear that both George Foster Peabody (financial supporter of both Hampton and Tuskegee) and Booker T. Washington were guests there. Beyond the "rhetoric" and "politics," however, Harper focuses finally on dinner table discussions of literature—Melville's *Moby-Dick*, perhaps, and the work of other Americans, contemporary and historic. Harper means as well his own work, no doubt. Had Washington's politics won out, Harper's oeuvre would not exist, including the poem under question. Washington's priority was economic enfranchisement, at the expense of both learning for its own sake and political enfranchisement; his emphasis on industrial education required that reading and writing be firmly linked to the learning of trades. Further, agriculture was to be the trade of choice at Tuskegee, with an eye to promoting higher crop yields and market production to ensure economic profit. In the words of one historian, who quotes Washington, "Instead of producing 'the proud fop with his beaver hat, kid gloves, and walking cane,' industrial education would return the rural youth to his home community unspoiled and dedicated to its uplift" (Harlan 161).

The Great Rainbowed Swamp

Harper's poems investigate the interrelationships among education, capitalism, and racism, grounding these questions specifically in a sense of place that recalls and interrogates Washington's role as the great enthusiast for social uplift for post–Civil War blacks. In *Working with the Hands*, Washington wrote, "Our pathway must be up through the soil, up through swamps, up through forests, up through the streams and rocks; up through commerce, education, and religion!" (29). His statement alludes to the linking of slavery (and therefore African Americans) with agriculture, and it invokes swamps as both literal challenges to successful farming and as figurative impediments to self- and race-improvement. It also suggests the figure of Etienne, who "went back to Africa as—a trader." Further, the relationship between land and commerce, past and future, and oppression and uplift that Washington assumes is the one that Harper examines, using some of the same language.

For Washington, swamps were a small part of the terrain over which the descendants of slaves must travel to achieve the transcendence of uplift. "Psychophotos of Hampton" presents more, and increasingly complicated, references to swamps: the "mosquitoed swamp near Fort Monroe" (29); "swampgrounds, campsites" (33); and the "literature of the great / rainbowed swamp" (144–45). Like the places from Sethe's past in Morrison's *Beloved*, which still exist despite intervals of time and distance, the swamps in Harper's poem are remnants from the continent's—and the nation's—past; yet they are still accessible as he "walks out" among them. For Harper, the swamp is both tenor and vehicle, a place of both natural and historical processes. His diction implies the importance of connotative and denotative nuance in the poem's moral ecology.

Not only among environmentalists, the term "wetland" has largely replaced "swampland," conferring a changed set of attitudes and political policies. The *Oxford English Dictionary* defines "swamp" as first occurring in reference to colonial North America, specifically Virginia; the combination "dismal swamp" was a frequent appellation for wet, low-lying regions, implying dreary and possibly evil connotations. Early uses of the term "swamp" suggest richness of soil yet unsuitability for agriculture. The history of the word, therefore, is woven with Anglo-colonial attitudes toward land—as a resource to be exploited, with any hindrances amounting to either negative costs on the balance sheet or divine evidence of Native American misuse.[5] "Wetland," however, shows the shift in attitude that results from the twentieth-century scarcity of swamp ecosystems. An 1847 usage of "wetland" reflects the utilitarian attitudes we saw with "swamp": "Wetland . . . by judicious cultivation . . . rapidly improves in fertility." Examples of usage from 1979, 1980, and 1985 show a swift progression of connotation, emphasizing "plans to protect the Somerset wetlands," intentions to "preserve this swamp area in its natural state . . . for wetland flora [and] birds and animals," and legal codification of those attitudes where "[u]nder state law construction cannot take place on a wetlands unless there are plans to replace the wetlands," respectively.

Harper's poem depicts the swamps, devoid of late political protections, as the literal testing grounds for American economic identity and race policy. Further, these swamps are indeed places of death and decay, ecological monuments to the past. Yet Harper identifies the kind of connection to the past that promises a future: spiritual or cultural "fertility." And like the places from Sethe's past that still exist, despite intervals of time and distance, these swamps from the nation's past are still accessible, as the poet "walks out" among them.

The poem's mansions are also still in existence, from the grounds of Yaddo to the Franklin Delano Roosevelt estate at Hyde Park (near, incidentally, the magnificent Vanderbilt estate) to Robert E. Lee's mansion at Arlington and back again to Yaddo. Significantly, Harper details aspects of their placement and history that connect to his contention that "the Renaissance [was] built on slave trading" and his interest in the connections among red and black people in North America. He refers to Roosevelt's mansion as being situated near Esopus, New York, a place named for the indigenous inhabitants, the Esopus (although it is usually called by the family's name, Springwood, or placed at Hyde Park). Harper notes that the handsome mansion at Arlington, built originally as a memorial to George Washington, "sprouted with Union graves" at the "doorstep" (36, 37) when Secretary of War Edwin Stanton approved General Montgomery Meigs's suggestion that the grounds become a military cemetery; a tomb containing 2,111 unknown soldiers was constructed in the estate's rose garden. Although the poem makes no mention of the fact, the grounds around Arlington became Freedman's Village, a camp for former slaves including not only a tent city but an industrial school aimed, like Tuskegee, at teaching trades. Initially located on low-lying land, a portion of the village was moved when its water supply was found to be contaminated by adjacent marshes (Peters 23–31). Harper does refer to Wiltwyk School for Boys, a home for troubled youth established on land the Roosevelt family donated. Again, the connection is implied between these young people and the young dead of the Native American graveyards such as that found at Hampton.[6]

Stark Black Dearth

The repeated contrast of swampland to mansion in "Psychophotos of Hampton" provides a structure both literal (evoking not only place names but the features of the land) and thematic (exploring the ironies and injustices of the historical devotion to trade). This connection, arising from Harper's interest in American history and the places it has played out, is one familiar to ecocritics from the work of Aldo Leopold, who, although his main focus is ecology, also suggests the linking of human morality—and commodification—with ecological outcomes. Leopold opens his famous essay "The Land Ethic" with a description of the ethical consequence of treating human beings as chattel, or property: the hanging of a dozen slave girls suspected of wrongdoing. "This hanging involved no question of propriety. The girls were property. The disposal of property was then, as now, a matter of expediency, not of right and wrong" (201).

Leopold looks back three thousand years to Odysseus and ancient Greece, but Harper reminds us that we need look no further than the nineteenth century and no farther than the land we inhabit. Harper also focuses more specifically on the ethical effects of capitalist commodification and the pursuit of economic profit, not merely the ethical questions of property rights. Leopold and Harper arrive at a similar viewpoint, despite their different directions of approach. Ecocritics would do well to consider the implications this convergence of ethics connotes.

First, we are reminded that issues of race in ecological theory or politics extend well beyond where landfills or toxic industries are located, although these are important factors. Second, and more important for literary studies, we must continue to develop the examinations of both genre and aesthetics for what Lawrence Buell defines as an "ecological text" (7–8). Even as critics have begun to note that inner-city and urban residents may not feel the appeal of wilderness literature, we should not inadvertently ghettoize black literature. Harper does not invoke W. E. B. Du Bois's notion of the "talented tenth" and its emphasis on fostering keen intellectual education for the "exceptional" rather than uniformly endorsing technical or industrial education for all. Yet the poems clearly share Du Bois's criticism of Washington's exclusive focus on industrial education, while they condemn the pursuit of capitalist profit.

Censure and praise both take shape in these poems through implication. As in the modernist tradition, Harper relies on juxtaposition and inference rather than rhetoric or narrative, and he demands an extraordinary amount of work from his readers. Indeed, much of the aesthetic body of each poem depends on its relation to other poems and the way a careful and informed reader will see connections and ironies. This technique is often seen as academic, but despite its inter- and intra-textual allusiveness, Harper reminds us that he does not live—or write—in an ivory tower. Although Harper may sometimes write with resonance to Ezra Pound or T. S. Eliot, he writes of Booker T. Washington and Etienne as well as all the fallen dead of Hampton Institute, Arlington, and beyond.

Herein lies Harper's important contribution to contemporary poetry, combining a modernist use of allusion with criticism of the cultural tenets that modernism so often endorsed. His is the "literature of the great / rainbowed swamp," and it recalls Robert Browning's poem "'Childe Roland to the Dark Tower Came'":

Names in my ears
Of all the lost adventurers my peers,—
How such a one was strong, and such was bold,
And such was fortunate, yet each of old
 Lost, lost! one moment knelled the woe of years.
 (194–99)

As the swamps provide natural monuments to the dead, the poem's allusions provide an elegiac structure that is based in history and literature; yet it is also bathed in private, personal detail. The Dark Tower implies contrast with the ivory tower academic writers are said to inhabit as well as correction to the leisured privilege of the Trask mansion. Who are "the lost adventurers my peers" for Harper? They are the dead—both black and Native American—who repeatedly surface, ghosts or conjured presences, throughout the poems. Not all are named as directly as the dead at Hampton. Harper's friend and fellow poet, the late Robert Hayden, joins him in "Psychophotos of Hampton," although most readers may not realize this. Harper says that he and Hayden visited the grounds of Hampton Institute together, and they stood under the Emancipation Tree as they talked about poetry.[7]

Standing in America's swamps, Harper may think of himself as a corrective to the Trasks' self-congratulating chivalry, surveying the surroundings like Browning's knight in "'Childe Roland to the Dark Tower Came'":

Then came a bit of stubbed ground, once a wood,
 Next a marsh, it would seem, and now mere earth
 Desperate and done with; (so a fool finds mirth,

Makes a thing and then mars it, till his mood
Changes and off he goes!) within a rood—
  Bog, clay and rubble, sand and stark black dearth.
  (145–50)

Yet the poem looks forward as well as back: Harper's oldest son is named Roland, as is the knight in Browning's poem.

Thus I find the poems in the "Uplift" series, despite their elegiac tendencies, to offer more hope than much of Harper's earlier work. The swamps are full of the submerged history of this nation, and Harper has made a point of quoting William Carlos Williams that this history "begins in murder and enslavement, not discovery" (*TriQuarterly* 119). However, the "great rainbowed swamp" is not the colorless swamp of Browning's poem. It is a site of aesthetic beauty, of unity among people of color, and of guarded promise. Beyond the "rubble" and "dearth" of Browning's dismal allegory, beyond the all-too-physical mire of Washington's symbolic obstacles, Harper's emphasis on the swamp's "literature" calls on readers to preserve the swamp's accumulation of memories. Place matters, he implies, both for itself and for the historic and emotional meaning it has accrued for people who lived and died there: Place can bear witness if we pay attention.

NOTES

1. Letter to the author in August 1999.

2. See "Healing Song" and "Psychophotos of Hampton" in *Images of Kin* 14, 34. For a treatment of the inclusion of African Americans in Native American tribes, see Katz.

3. The major towns of Providence and Newport indicated the importance of trade in defining the economy and land use patterns of the colony (and then the state). The effects on forest and big game due to colonial-British trade exchange was similar to the rest of New England: by 1850 the tree cover of Rhode Island had been reduced from 95 percent to 32 percent. The beaver fur trade decimated not only the beaver population but also species who depended on the beaver-pond ecosystems for survival. Specific to Rhode Island, changes in the land were distinctly linked to the seaport emphasis on trade. By 1828, the Blackstone canal was constructed along the Blackstone River to connect Wooster with Providence and Newport. See Merchant 66–67, 193–95, 225.

4. In "The Battle of Saratoga" (Springs) Revisited," Harper mentions "a private printing / of a history of *Yaddo*" (*Images of Kin* 3–4).

5. The *Oxford English Dictionary* cites Captain John Smith in Virginia, 1624: "Some small Marshes and Swamps there are, but more profitable than hurtfull."

6. In a telephone conversation with this author, Harper said, "I feel certain that the land is an old Indian graveyard," although I have been unable to confirm his claim.

7. Telephone call with the author in May 1997.

Works Cited

Bailyn, Bernard. *The New England Merchants in the Seventeenth Century.* Cambridge: Harvard UP, 1955,

Browning, Robert. *The Poems.* Ed. John Pettigrew, Vol. 1. New Haven: Yale UP, 1981.

Buell, Lawrence. *The Environmental Imagination: Thoreau, Nature Writing, and the Formation of American Culture.* Cambridge: Belknap–Harvard P, 1995.

Coughtry, James. *The Notorious Triangle: Rhode Island and the African Slave Trade, 1700–1807.* Philadelphia: Temple UP, 1981.

Du Bois, W. E. B. *The Souls of Black Folk.* New York: Random House, 1996.

Evernden, Neil. "Beyond Ecology: Self, Place, and the Pathetic Fallacy." Glotfelty and Fromm 92–104.

Gaustad, Edwin S. *Liberty of Conscience: Roger Williams in America.* Grand Rapids: William B. Eerdmans, 1991.

Glotfelty, Cheryll, and Harold Fromm, eds. *The Ecocriticism Reader: Landmarks in Literary Ecology.* Athens: U of Georgia P, 1996.

Harlan, Louis R. *Booker T. Washington: The Making of a Black Leader, 1856–1901.* New York: Oxford UP, 1972.

Harper, Michael S. *Dear John, Dear Coltrane.* Pittsburgh: U of Pittsburgh P, 1970.

———. *Debridement* Garden City: Doubleday, 1973.

———. *History as Apple Tree.* San Francisco: Scarab, 1972.

———. *History Is Your Own Heartbeat.* Urbana: U of Illinois P, 1971.

———. *Honorable Amendments.* Urbana: U of Illinois P, 1995.

———. *Images of Kin: New and Selected Poems.* Urbana: U of Illinois P, 1977.

———. Interview with David Lloyd. *TriQuarterly* 65 (winter 1986): 119–28.

———. Letter to the author. 13 August 1999.

———. *Nightmare Begins Responsibility.* Urbana: U of Illinois P, 1975.

———. *Song: I Want a Witness.* Pittsburgh: U of Pittsburgh P, 1972.

———. Telephone interview. 31 May 1997.

Jeffers, Robinson. *The Double Axe and Other Poems.* 1948. New York: Liverwright, 1977.

Katz, William Loren. *Black Indians: A Hidden Heritage.* New York: Atheneum, 1986.

Kolodny, Annette. *The Lay of the Land: Metaphor as Experience and History in American Life and Letters.* Chapel Hill: U of North Carolina P, 1975.

Leopold, Aldo. *A Sand County Almanac and Sketches Here and There.* New York: Oxford UP, 1987.

Love, Glen A. "Revaluing Nature: Toward an Ecological Criticism." Glotfelty and Fromm 225–40.

Lutwack, Leonard. *The Role of Place in Literature.* Syracuse: Syracuse UP, 1984.

Merchant, Carolyn. *Ecological Revolutions: Nature, Gender, and Science in New England.* Chapel Hill: U of North Carolina P, 1989.

Miller, Perry. *Roger Williams: His Contribution to the American Tradition.* New York: Atheneum, 1962.

Morrison, Toni. *Beloved.* New York: Knopf, 1987.

Peters, James Edward. *Arlington National Cemetery: Shrine to America's Heroes.* Kensington, MD: Woodbine, 1986.

Snyder, Gary. *The Practice of the Wild.* San Francisco: North Point, 1990.

Trask, Kate [Katrina] Nichols. *Yaddo: The Story of Yaddo.* Privately printed. Boston: The Thomas Todd Co., 1923.

Washington, Booker T. *Working with the Hands.* 1904. New York: Arno, 1969.

ZOFIA BURR

Maya Angelou on the Inaugural Stage

Whether one is dealing with Emily Dickinson's letter-poems to Susan Gilbert Dickinson, Josephine Miles's anti-Vietnam War poetry, Gwendolyn Brooks's black power poetry, or Audre Lorde's poetry about the politics of difference, there's a consistent tendency to devalue the poetry as prosaic, propagandistic, or journalistic or to interpret it as narrowly autobiographical, expressive of personal experience and sensibility rather than engaged with the poet's—and the reader's—world. By focusing on the dynamics of address, we have seen how Miles, Brooks, and Lorde elaborate poetic practices that escape the confines of the personal and how each of them articulates, in her own way, a "women's poetry" that engages with the politics of the public world. As she works out an idiom that can make of poetry a genre interested in communicative utterance, each of these poets contends with the powerful prescriptions about what constitutes poetic merit and with pervasive expectations about the character of poetry by women. Miles, Brooks, and Lorde have been regularly misunderstood and marginalized as poets; they do not figure in any of the larger narratives about twentieth-century American poetry. In examining their careers and reading their poems, I have offered some ways of rethinking our commonplace assumptions about women, poetry, and politics. But by attending extensively to the actual reception of poetry by women across this century in the United States, I have found little evidence to encourage optimism about the state of our thinking about these issues. Maya Angelou's poem for the presidential inauguration in 1993 can serve as a kind of coda to my argument.

First known in the literary world for her best-selling autobiographies, Angelou (b. 1928) has become probably the most widely recognized poet in contemporary U.S. culture. She is found on television, in the movies, on the radio, in print, on the lecture circuit, on the Internet, at the 1993 presidential inauguration, and at the Million Man March. Given this extraordinary career, she also serves as an exemplary figure, the reception of whose work allows us to discern some of the complications and impasses that attend us when we seek to examine a poetry that is unabashedly public in its ambitions.

The role of inaugural poet, positioning the poet as a nationally representative public voice, conflicts fundamentally with dominant conceptions of poetry, its purposes, and its character as a linguistic practice. This concluding discussion serves to underline some of the concerns this project has raised about the possible uses of poetry and about avenues for critical response opened up by attention to poetry as utterance and performance, to the poet's person and persona, and to audience and poetic address.

Poet and Public

Angelou's failure to impress professional poetry critics has always been linked to her success with a larger public audience. For instance, in a review of Angelou's 1976 collection, *Oh Pray My Wings Are Gonna Fit Me Well*, James Finn Cotter describes the book as an "unfortunate example" of the "dangers of success."[1] He argues that Angelou's access and responsiveness to the public have muted the private and personal quality that he takes to be essential to poetry. In Angelou's poetry, he argues, "the public voice drowns out the private emotion" (103). Cotter suggests that when Angelou writes with an ear to the oral presentation of the poem, she is writing for a public audience; by contrast, when she writes for its reception by a solitary reader, she is able to be true to the "private emotion" that is the source of good poetry. "Too many public readings may prove the undoing of the *personal* voice," Cotter suggests. "What wows an audience may offend on the printed page" (104; my emphasis). There is a striking difference between the sensibilities attributed to the auditor and to the reader of poetry in this assertion. The remark speaks to that most modern and western of our poetic prejudices, construing poetry as a written genre, the difficulties and interests of which respond to the attentions of the private reader rather than the face-to-face public auditor. The audience member who responds to the oral presentation of poetry is criticized for not knowing (or not caring) that he or she is responding to a poetry in which what is valuable is "drowned" or submerged. And Angelou's critics do nothing more energetically than dismiss the people who value her poetry.

In 1971, John Alfred Avant, for instance, deliberately insults the taste of those readers who like the poetry in *Just Give Me a Cool Drink of Water 'fore I Diiie*: "there will be an audience for this rather well done schlock poetry, not to be confused with poetry for people who read poetry. . . . This collection isn't accomplished, not by any means; but some readers are going to love it."[2] The point of Cotter's and Avant's remarks is clearly not to instruct the audience whose sensibilities are in question. The reviews do not address them; Angelou's readers are presumed, in any case, not to be readers of such reviews. As Joanne Braxton points out, "Angelou's audience, composed largely of women and blacks, isn't really affected by what white and/or male critics of the dominant literary tradition have to say about her work. This audience does not read literary critics; it does read Maya Angelou."[3] Comments critical of Angelou's audience are addressed to readers outside of that audience and designed to confirm us in our sense that Angelou is not an interesting poet and that we are discerning readers.

Even critics who value poetry as an oral tradition have nonetheless found Angelou wanting. Their terms reveal the extent to which they also privilege an intimate poetic "voice" as the essential constituent of good poetry. In an article linked to several Maya Angelou web sites, Bryan D. Bourn attributes her "success as a writer" to her use of the "oral tradition of many African tribes."[4] Bourn argues that "Angelou slips into banality when she abandons [these traditions], which is frequently the case in her poetry." "When she strays from [the African oral tradition], her writing gets flatter, less emotional. To put it simply, we no longer hear Angelou's '*voice*.'" Bourn associates this "voice" with what he identifies as a "conversational tone" and "immediacy of feeling."

Bourn posits a poetic voice whose source of vitality is identical with that which kills the poetic voice by Cotter's definition—the oral context. Nevertheless, Bourn's privileging of the emotional is closely connected to Cotter's sense of the private. In both cases, the expectation is that the poet's voice is an intimate, personal voice. We see this more clearly when Bourn points to those rare "examples in Angelou's poetry where her 'voice' does come through," that is, in the "poems relating *personal* experience" (my emphasis).[5] From the perspective of the critic privileging the written context, the poet must be an individual speaking as if to herself; from the perspective of the critic privileging the oral context, she must be speaking to and for her people.

Like Cotter, Bourn faults Angelou for going public, but not because she has left the garret for the soapbox. Instead, he faults her for turning away from her more immediate community to address a general audience. What neither critic thinks worth exploring is that to do this, she has, in places, taken a stance that is meant to be representative rather than individual, authoritative rather than confessional—most strikingly, of course, in her 1993 inaugural poem, "On the Pulse of Morning." The narrowness of Cotter's and Bourn's conceptions of poetry means that, for them and many other like-minded critics, Angelou's acceptance of the role of inaugural poet was bound to end in failure. Yet the decision to appoint an inaugural poet was only made in light of John F. Kennedy's success with Robert Frost as inaugural poet in 1961. Examining the response to Frost's inaugural performance more closely, however, reveals that his "success" was ambiguous at best and not necessarily that different from Angelou's perceived failure.

Inaugural Poets

When it made the news in late 1992 that Maya Angelou had been asked to read a poem at Clinton's upcoming inauguration, commentators inevitably compared her role as inaugural poet to that of Robert Frost at John F. Kennedy's 1961 inauguration. Frost had been the first poet ever to deliver a poem at an American presidential inauguration, and Angelou was the second.[6] Newspaper and magazine articles that compared the two poets underlined the differences in their racial and gender identities and asserted an ostensibly uncomplicated narrative of social progress in the fact that a "black woman" would be standing in the place of a "white man,"[7] occupying a representative role that, in the earlier era, it would have been hard to imagine anyone other than a white man fulfilling.

Angelou herself made the comparison with Frost. But unlike her contemporaries' accounts of Frost's reading, her account focuses on the identification she felt with Frost as a result of the difficulty he encountered in trying to read his prefatory poem. Although Frost had written a prefatory poem for the occasion to accompany "The Gift Outright," the sun's glare made it too difficult for him to read it, and after struggling with a few lines he decided to forgo it and simply recite the poem "The Gift Outright," which he knew by heart. Recalling this scene, Angelou says: "Robert Frost was such a fine poet.... He was white and male, but he stood for me, and for Spanish people and Chinese people.... He was old and soon to die and couldn't see his own notes. He had the moxie to push on and recite what he knew. That further endeared him to me."[8] Angelou directs us away from the differences between herself and Frost. She doesn't say that she sees Frost's white maleness as an impasse in his capacity to represent her; rather, she focuses on his "moxie" and his mortality as traits that made him dear to her.

That Angelou reads Frost's triumph over his temporary vulnerability on the inaugural stage as a sign of his capacity to represent much more than himself is of a piece with journalistic coverage at the time of the event. Reporting on the Kennedy inauguration, the press in 1961 repeatedly turns Frost's difficulties at the podium, and his overcoming those difficulties, into a figure for the resilience of the nation and, in the context of Kennedy's inaugural address, of the resilience of the nation under the pressures of the cold war. *Life* magazine's coverage of the Kennedy inauguration makes the analogy most explicit by applying what Frost's (unread) dedication says about the nation's struggles to Frost's struggle to read the dedication itself: "In an affecting episode during the inaugural ceremonies, Robert Frost, 86, the patriarchal New England poet, received the undivided sympathy of the distinguished gathering. Frost, who had been asked by Kennedy to render his celebrated poem, 'The Gift Outright,' had thoughtfully written a dedicatory preface to the new President. But as the winter sun flared over his manuscript, Frost muttered, 'I can't see in this light.' Finally he gave up the attempt to read it. Frost was true, however, to two lines in his preface which he never got to: 'The turbulence we're in the middle of / Is something we can hardly help but love.' Dignified in his distress, he recited 'The Gift Outright,' which he knew by heart in a voice that was rich and strong."[9] Here we see how, in a sense, whatever was personal about Frost's struggle accrued a public meaning by virtue of its occurrence in a public (and highly ritualized) setting. Frost may have been trying, hardily, to read a written text, but his performance was rescripted by commentators as a "scene" in a larger narrative of international tensions and rivalry. Or, given its airing on television, it might be described as an "episode" in an unfolding story of politics and public culture. Ultimately, the meaning of Frost's inaugural reading, as reflected in its reception, was focused more on the context in which it occurred than on the poem itself.

Though at the time, Frost's person, poem, and dilemma were accepted as representative, expressive of the various vulnerabilities and struggles faced by Americans since 1942 when "The Gift Outright" was first published, retrospectively, Frost himself has not been considered "representative" of the people, nor has his representation of the nation in "The Gift Outright" been considered honest by later commentators. The poem locates the nation in the relationship between the "land" and the prerevolutionary Anglo settler, eliding the devastation to Native American and African cultures upon which the new nation silently depends and focusing instead on the bond between the land and "us".[10]

> The land was ours before we were the land's.
> She was our land more than a hundred years
> Before we were her people. She was ours
> In Massachusetts, in Virginia,

But we were England's, still colonials,
Possessing what we were still unpossessed by,
Possessed by what we now no more possessed.
Something we were withholding made us weak
Until we found out that it was ourselves
We were withholding from our land of living,
And forthwith found salvation in surrender.
Such as we were we gave ourselves outright
(The deed of gift was many deeds of war)
To the land vaguely realizing westward,
But still unstoried, artless, unenhanced,
Such as she was, such as she would become.[11]

Though the poem is in places ambiguous in tone ("The deed of gift was many deeds of war"), contemporary readers tend to be quick to distance themselves from what is frequently taken as an unambiguous celebration of "expansionism based on violence," to use the words of the *Washington Post* from January 1993.

There has thus been a nearly complete reversal in the perception of Frost's representativeness as inaugural poet, and this transformation marks the changes in cultural perceptions and cultural politics in the last thirty years.[12] The repeated event of a poet reading at a presidential inauguration, however, unearths a tension between the representativeness and the individuality of the poet's voice that has persisted in the reception of modern poetry in the United States. The occasion of the inaugural poem resurrects an ideology about the role of poetry in the public sphere that is as influential now as it was in the early 1960s. Kennedy's views on the value of the poet as the voice of the private individual, the voice of individual integrity over and against all the compromises and distortions of public discourses and institutions—including the state as the prototypical public institution—nicely illuminates the perceived incompatibility of the true poet as individual voice and poetry as a public idiom.

Prompted by Interior Secretary Stewart L. Udall, Kennedy's decision to invite a poet to read at his inauguration underlined his frequently stated belief that the responsible exercise of political power requires the resistance of the arts. In the terms Kennedy used at the dedication of the Robert Frost Library at Amherst College in October 1963 (after Frost's death in January of that year), the politicians are "the men who create power," while the artists are the men "who question power."[13] In this configuration, the artists provide a check on those who hold political power in much the same way political protest and "freedom of speech," in a democracy, are considered a check on elected representatives. Kennedy states: "When power corrupts, poetry cleanses. For art establishes the basic human truths which must serve as the touchstones of our judgement. The artist, however faithful to his personal vision of reality, becomes the last champion of the individual mind and sensibility against an intrusive society and an officious state" (136). But even as Kennedy criticizes the state for being "officious," he makes it clear that a society that allows or encourages the artist to fulfill his function as "champion of the individual mind" is far superior to a society that would require the artist to fulfill some other function. "In free society," Kennedy asserts, "art is not a weapon, and it does not belong to the sphere of polemics and ideology. Artists are not engineers of the soul. It may be different elsewhere. But [in a] democratic society . . . the highest duty of the writer . . . is to remain true to himself and to let the chips fall where they may" (136). By "elsewhere," Kennedy obviously means the Soviet Union and other communist states. And that the American artist is free "to let the chips fall where they may" is an obvious and familiar cold-war assertion of our superiority.

This sense of the independence of the artist in America, however, has a history that extends before the cold war and has also been defined in contrast to the relationship between the British monarch and his or her Poet Laureate.[14] In accord with national sentiment, no president of the United States would want it said that he honored a poet for the sake of having the occasions of his state or his rule praised in return. In fact, about a month after Kennedy's inauguration, a *New York Times* writer took the opportunity to distinguish this president's relationship to his inaugural poet from the English monarch's relationship with the Poet Laureate: "We have not and cannot have a national poet laureate, but we do need poets who without flattering us tell us how to face danger and how to conquer it. It is a good sign that President Kennedy recognizes this function of the poet."[15] Kennedy's perspective acknowledges a public role for poetry, but only insofar as it remains untouched by the public world or public commitments, only insofar as poetry's public is based on its private orientation.

The function of the poet as a check on power is both analogous to that of the press as the Fourth Estate (understood as having a responsibility to scrutinize the actions of the government from the perspective of the people) and also absolutely unlike the press, insofar as the press remains part of the public sphere and its imperatives—the very things that poetry is designed to check and counter in the name of integrity defined in terms of the private, the personal, the individual. Thus, if poetry has a public role to perform it is only by virtue of and on the basis of its ability to remain an idiom apart from all the public discourses of society. By this account, the maker of the poem cannot anticipate a public role for his or her work and have it remain poetry.

In this light, Frost's failure to read the verse he wrote for the occasion of the inauguration preserved his integrity as a poet. (In fact, subsequent critical commentary on the unread "Dedication" tends to refer to it as "a lamentable work.")[16] "The Gift Outright," which he did read, was already an authentic poem; now it was being overheard at the inauguration—a legitimate, because accidental or unanticipated, transition onto the stage of national politics. The poem's status as a genuine poem was never put into question. But Angelou's poem "On the Pulse of Morning," conceived and unveiled as an inaugural poem, is read in the suspicious light of public discourse. And having taken form as a poem designed to grace the inaugural stage, it must subsequently seek an afterlife as a genuine poem—a very different and hugely fraught (perhaps impossible) transition.

When it came time to tell the stories that Angelou's presence at the inauguration licensed us to tell about ourselves as "American" people, no one in the liberal press disputed Angelou's representativeness or the appropriateness of such a gesture of inclusion on the Clinton administration's part.[17] But the response to the poem as a poem uncovered and raised literary anxieties to a fever pitch. At its most politely critical, the evaluation of the poem was phrased as a question of genre. As the poet David Lehman put it: "If you define her task as a theatrical one, she did what was expected. If you define her task as a political one, she did what was expected. But if you ask me as a poet to be as ruthless on this poem as I would be on any other, I would have to say it's not very memorable."[18]

From Lehman's account, "as a poet," what we learn about (what counts as) poetic discourse is that it is not theatrical or political discourse. Instead, it is an ascetic idiom that eschews such forms of popularity and public engagement. But the fact that Lehman applies all three categories to Angelou's presentation suggests that while the political, theatrical, and poetic may be theoretically extricable, in this instance they are intertwined. Perhaps the most important thing about Lehman's response to Angelou's poem as a poem is the distance his poetic purism puts between him and the poem's multivalent function in the context of the inauguration. This distance makes the utterance available for narrowly literary evaluation rather than any other kind of response: the question of the poem's literary quality comes to be divorced from its substantive content and manner and is treated as an autonomous aspect of the poem, separate from its political and performative impact.[19]

The question of whether or not Angelou's poem fulfilled the auditor's expectations or requirements for a good poem became so important for some commentators that it overwhelmed the poem's politics. In Ishmael Reed's response, for instance, the length of the poem becomes more important than its argument: "'Frost's poem is the last gasp of the settler sensibility. It says the country was created so it could be occupied by Europeans. "The Gift Outright" [however] has the advantage of being short—only 16 lines. Angelou took the risk of going more than six times that length. I always taught my students to stick to 12 lines. You just can't win when you write a long poem."[20] It's possible, of course, that coming from Reed—a writer known for irony and parody—these comments represent his parody of an academic poet's perspective as much as (or more than) they represent his own perspective. Nevertheless, sincere or parodic, they are a good representation of narrowly "literary" responses to poetry and the way in which such responses can celebrate a poem that endorses colonialist domination by focusing on its brevity and concision and can damn another poem by invoking a categorical objection to long poems. The separation of literary from ethicopolitical concerns is here subjected to a kind of reductio ad absurdum.

Even as the length of the poem is at issue, so is the fact that it is a poem made on this occasion to be performed and heard rather than to wait silently for its reader. For many commentators, what counts as poetic richness and complexity must be distinguished from any complexity that would be the effect of the context of performance. As Sterling Plumpp puts it, expressing an opinion that was repeatedly articulated, "At the level of a public poem, which is performed, I think it's brilliant. I'm not quite as enthusiastic about it as a text."[21] Among the most diplomatic to make this distinction between "public poem" and poetic "text" was Rita Dove, who said: "'I wouldn't compare it to a poem I'll read over and over again in silence. That's not the kind of poem it was meant to be. It's a song, really.'"[22] Dove's comment taps into that commonplace of critical discourse that if a poem is good, it is worth returning to "over and over again." It draws on the assumption that a poem is meant to be read silently and in private because what counts as poetic richness and complexity must be distinguished, as I have suggested, from any complexity that would be the effect of the context of performance. Indeed, if the performance of a poem is particularly striking, and if a poem seems to depend on its performance for its power, then it is not as highly valued as a poem. So the quality of the speaking voice itself—the instrument for which the poem might be said to be written—can be read as a suggestion of the poem's lack. Louise Erdrich offers praise of Angelou's reading that serves to belittle and disregard the poem in just this manner: "'I felt that this woman could have read the side of a cereal box,'" she comments. "'Her presence was so powerful and momentous.'"[23]

This kind of backhanded compliment was not, however, meted out to Frost's recitation of "The Gift Outright." No one took his capacity to recite the poem "in a voice that was rich and strong" as a sign of the inadequacy of the poem itself. Frost's powerful reading served to supplement the poem in the sense of enhancing it, while Angelou's powerful reading of her poem supplemented it in the sense of making evident its inadequacy and lack. A prime reason for the differences between these articulations of the trouble with poetry in the public sphere has to do with the fact that the notion of the "public" is always already gendered and racialized. So the ideology making it difficult for a poet to speak with anything other than a private voice will bear unevenly, sometimes contradictorily, on women and men, nonwhites and whites. With regards to the reception of Angelou's poetry in particular, because our assumptions about the private nature of women's voices heighten our expectation that women poets will speak out of a place that is private and intimate at the same time that our expectations about nonwhite poets suggest that they should speak for "their people," as their representative, the bridge between the work of an African American woman poet and the notion of a general public is especially fragile.

The assumptions about poetic idiom at work in these negative responses to Angelou's poem are not, of course, fully shared by all American poets. Ntozake Shange's response to Angelou's poem clearly has more to do with its performativity and its affective impact than with whether or not it fulfills expectations of the genre of poetry: "'I think ["On the Pulse of Morning"] is going to sustain me now. My father just died the other day, and I really needed some sustenance. I got it from her.'" And Shange goes on to suggest the way in which Angelou's poem, even as it provides personal sustenance in a time of loss, provides sustenance at the more explicitly political or national level. "'[F]or the first time since I was on the Mall for an anti-war rally in 1969 have I felt so moved as to actually want to be here now in this country.'"[24] Shange does not separate the poem from the context in which it functioned and does not separate the poetic from the political or the dramatic. In fact, she compares the presentation of Angelou's poem not to another poem but to another situation in which public utterance functioned as political protest.

What all of the responses to Angelou's poem neglect, however, is the multiplicity of ways in which Angelou's inaugural poem speaks back to Frost's inaugural poems. By focusing on the contrasts between Angelou's and Frost's poems, the intertextual dialogue between the two poems is elided from view, as is the underlying continuity of the conceptions of poetic integrity and literary quality evident in the public discourse about poetry in 1961 and in 1993. Angelou's poem, at one level, rewrites Frost's "The Gift Outright" (and his prefatory poem "For John F. Kennedy His Inauguration"), revisiting some of its commonplaces from another perspective, and in so doing, it also seeks to refashion some of our assumptions about the purposes of public poetry, rearticulating the inflection of national panegyric.

Angelou's poem returns to the scene of the European colonization of America treated by "The Gift Outright." But instead of speaking from the (expected) "human," "American" perspective, Angelou's poem offers as its main speakers "I, the Rock, I, the River, I, the Tree." Through these voices, "the land" of Frost's poem speaks back to colonizer and colonized. Playing as they do on their meanings in black American spirituals, Angelou's animation of the rock of "No hiding place," the river of "Down by the riverside," and the tree of "I shall not be moved" articulates a "land" imbued with a specific history of oppression.[25] While Frost's poem constructs its inaugural moment as the founding of an American identity by instituting a break with the English past, Angelou repeats but transforms this gesture by alluding to the devastation of Native American and African cultures on which the founding of American culture depends and by highlighting the presence of non-Anglo communities in American culture. The history of the relation between the people and the land is still something of a matter of "possessing" and being "possessed," but not in the vaguely psychological sense of Frost's poem; rather, the history is rendered in terms of the stealing, buying, and selling of land and peoples. Unlike Frost's poem, in which the cost of the creation of the nation remains abstract and ambiguous, Angelou's poem represents the "Tree" as speaking to all the descendants of these cultures as persons for whom a significant *price* has been paid: "Each of you, descendant of some passed-/ On traveler, has been paid for" (271).

For Angelou as for Frost, a new beginning is to be inaugurated by a break with the past, but the "break" is only possible once the past is faced "with courage": "History, despite its wrenching pain, / Cannot be unlived, but if faced / With courage, need not be lived again" (272). Frost, in his prefatory poem for "The Gift Outright," states that "Heroic deeds were done" in the European conquest of the Americas and suggests that the subsequent rise of the U.S. polity established "a new order of ages"; he identifies this inaugural era of the past as an age of "glory" and the present as presaging "The glory of a next Augustan age / . . . / A golden age of poetry and power." For Frost, the stance of the Kennedy era, confronting the new frontier and the challenges it poses, allows "us" to reconnect with the outlook and ambitions of the era of the founding fathers; it allows "us" to relive that glorious history. Angelou revisits the terrain of Frost's inaugural poems, but only to confront the past, not to relive it. She too speaks of a new day dawning, of "a dream" waiting to be realized, but for her such a new age belongs not to the nation "we" have become but to the nation we have *yet* to become.

Most insistently, however, in a gesture related to the gesture of Lorde's "For Each of You," Angelou's poem places the responsibility for the future in the hands of its auditors by calling upon them specifically. Animating the voices of the Rock, River, and Tree throughout to evoke and call upon specific communities among a diverse and divided United States, Angelou's poem recognizes

> The African, the Native American, the Sioux,
> The Catholic, the Muslim, the French, the Greek,
> The Irish, the Rabbi, the Priest, the Sheik,
> The Gay, the Straight, the Preacher,
> The privileged, the homeless, the Teacher (271)

as they "hear / The speaking of the Tree" (271) as it tells us to "shape" "the dream" (272) in that "space" the "horizon" of a new day offers us "To place new steps of change" (273). That the poem (here and throughout) acknowledges the many "Americans" that Frost's poem elides is certainly an important aspect of its impact. And insofar as that acknowledgment testifies to the changes in our understanding of American culture, it marks a significant development in the complexity of our self-understanding.

Angelou calls on each of her auditors to take the dream that sustains them and to "Mold it into the shape of your most / Private need. Sculpt it into / The image of your most public self" (272). She argues for a world in which "private need" and "public self" enter into a kind of consonance rather than simply celebrating private integrity as a check on the public sphere. Unlike Frost in his prefatory verses for the inauguration, Angelou never directly addresses the president or the politicians in her inaugural poem. Her words carry an admonition to "study war no more" (rejecting the "many deeds of war" that "The Gift Outright" identifies as our primary "deed of gift" to "our" new land), but her poem's address is directed elsewhere and otherwise—from the land itself to the many peoples who have sought harbour there, "Each of you" (271). Angelou's most significant rewriting of Frost is to adopt a stance that eliminates entirely the compact and homogenous, the complacent "we" and "our" of Frost's inaugural poems. And she does this not by abandoning Frost's chosen ground but by reversing the perspective from which it is viewed and relocating her auditors in relation to it.

In addition to Frost's inaugural poems, "On the Pulse of Morning" gathers up strands from such poems as Walt Whitman's "Song of Myself" and Langston Hughes's "The Negro Speaks of Rivers" to construct a poem that was, to judge by its brisk sales as a booklet and audiotape, resonant for many Americans, however much it was lambasted or patronized by professional poets. The response of the poets and critics to Angelou's poem has, however, its own significance in light of my concerns in this study. By comparing some of the public responses to Angelou's performance of "On the Pulse of Morning" at Bill Clinton's inauguration in 1993 with some of the responses to Frost's performance of "The Gift Outright" at Kennedy's inauguration in 1961, we have seen how unevenly, but determinedly, we continue to decontextualize poetry, defining it as private, personal, individual, and antipublic, or defining it (which amounts to much the same thing) as "literary," as divorced from political and performative engagements. Thus, the presence of poetry at an American president's inauguration is at once an occasion on which poetry can be said to speak to an audience far broader than the academic and elite audiences that are often its selected cohorts and, at the same time, an exceptional appearance of poetry in public discourse—in response to which critics insistently reinscribed the generic boundaries separating genuine poetry, a public idiom, and a mass audience.

Poetic Justice

In John Singleton's film *Poetic Justice*,[26] the title character, Justice (played by Janet Jackson), is presented as the author of five previously published poems by Maya Angelou.[27] The presence of Angelou's poetry in this movie is yet another example of the wide circulation her work has enjoyed in contemporary American culture, and Singleton's movie seems, on the face of it, a cultural text in which poetry might be seen to have some kind of public function in relation to a broad audience. Such expectations are, however, quickly dispelled. For the most part, the poems enter the movie as voiceovers, spoken in Justice's voice as if she were composing them and serving as sound bridges across visual sequences. At only one point in the movie—when we see Justice reading a poem to her friend, Iesha—does the voice of the poet come from within the frame of the scene in which it is heard. Only on this occasion does it constitute diagetic sound, forming part of the action of the scene, rather than remaining a kind of commentary on the action that exists at one remove from the intersubjective world of the filmed scenario.[28]

Throughout the movie, Justice is represented as a private poet, writing to ease her own pain (after the loss of her murdered boyfriend). One critic describes her poetry writing as "therapy."[29] Justice is a young hairstylist who witnesses her boyfriend's murder at the beginning of the movie and has withdrawn from the world of relationships as a result—at least until Lucky, played by the rapper Tupac Shakur, draws her out. By casting the popular recording artists Janet Jackson and Tupac Shakur in the lead roles, Singleton implicitly raises generic questions about who counts as a poet and what counts as poetry.[30] Jackson, as Justice, writes poetry and Shakur, as Lucky, plays a young postal worker who aspires to rap. The presence of the rapper and the expectation that the audience will read his public image onto the movie role is further underlined by the fact that Justice and Lucky listen to and discuss rap recorded by Lucky's cousin. The tension created by the disparity between the status of the discourses of "poetry," "pop song," and "rap" is implicit in the casting and explicit as a struggle between the two main characters. At one point, Lucky asks Justice: "What you write about in that notebook you carry around?" She answers: "Ah, that's my poetry." Somewhat unexpectedly, the word "poetry" makes Lucky defensive. He responds: "You trying to say my cousin's shit ain't poetry?" She says, "Yeah it ain't if he ain't got nothin deep to say; gotta have a voice, and perspective." The exchange between these two characters potentially repositions poetry as one in a series of "spoken word" genres of performance, but the criterion that Justice invokes—it's not poetry if it doesn't have a personal, individual "voice"—returns us to the generic expectations that have accrued to poetry as a private and written art. I'd like to be able to argue that, by virtue of poetry's use as voiceover throughout, Singleton's movie accords poetry a public role—especially in those places where as a result of its juxtaposition with scenes of public strife it serves as a kind of social commentary. But within this movie there is little explicit acknowledgment of the poetry having anything other than a purely private and personal resonance; Justice, in particular, seems unaware even of the possibility that her poetry could have a more public dimension. Thus, even though Singleton's movie links Angelou's poetry with the popular genre of rap, it does so in a way that reinscribes poetry as an essentially private and personal affair. To the extent that a public idiom and intention are attached to "poetic" speech, they are constellated around the genre of rap and the figure of the rapper. In this movie, the public and private personae of the poet are divided between the gangsta rapper (who is decidedly masculinized) and the woman poet (who is equally emphatically feminized), thus confirming the expectations about women's poetry as private, personal, and autobiographical we have seen repeated time and again.

Despite the very different occasions of Angelou's reception that I have touched on—literary critical commentary on her published work, responses to her performance at the 1993 inauguration, and incorporation of her work into the mass medium of movies—there are surprisingly constant assumptions about the nature of poetry and its essential incompatibility with public engagements operating across all of these terrains. If we are dealing with a literary-critical prejudice, fostered by the academy and the poetry establishment, it turns out to be a prejudice that is widely disseminated. So much so, in fact, that even the very visible career of our most public poet at some of its most public moments has served only to reinscribe the assumed incompatibility of poetry and the public sphere.

NOTES

1. James Finn Cotter, review of *Oh Pray My Wings Are Gonna Fit Me Well*, by Maya Angelou, *Angel of Ascent*, by Robert Hayden, and *The Women and the Men*, by Nikki Giovanni, in *America*, 7 Feb. 1976, 103–4. Subsequent references appear parenthetically in the text. Sandra Gilbert also argues that fame has weakened Angelou's poetry. See "A Platoon of Poets," review of *Oh Pray My Wings Are Gonna Fit Me Well*, by Maya Angelou, and of books by Rosemary Daniell, Kenneth Koch, Diane Wakoski, Norman Dubie, and Etta Blum, in *Poetry* 128 (1976): 290–99.

2. John Alfred Avant, review of *Just Give Me a Cool Drink of Water 'fore I Diiie*, by Maya Angelou, in *Library Journal* 96 (1971): 3329

3. Joanne M. Braxton, "Maya Angelou," in *Modern American Women Writers: Profiles of Their Lives and Works, from the 1870s to the Present*, ed. Lea Baechler, Elaine Showalter, and A. Walton Litz (New York: Macmillan, 1993), 7.

4. Bryan D. Bourn, "Maya Angelou and the African-American Tradition," <http://www.usinternet.com/maya.htm>.

5. "There are examples in Angelou's poetry where her 'voice' does come through. Her narrative poems and poems relating personal experience, both tend to be more successful because they allow Maya to use her talent for storytelling that makes her prose work so successful" (ibid.).

6. Miller Williams was the third inaugural poet, reading "Of History and Hope" at the 1997 Clinton inaugural. Roy P. Basler notes, "The only precedent in American history, so far as I know, for a poet's elevation to the inaugural platform was Adlai's [Stevenson's] selection of Carl [Sandburg] to perform the ancient duty of ruler's chosen bard, at his inauguration as Governor of Illinois in 1948" (*The Muse and the Librarian* [Westport, Conn.: Greenwood Press, 1974], 75).

7. See, for example, Janet Cawley, "Poet Aims to Capture Spirit of America," *Chicago Tribune*, 19 Jan. 1993, 6; and Irvin Molotsky, "Poet of the South for the Inauguration," *New York Times*, 5 Dec. 1992, A8+.

8. Molotsky, "Poet of the South for the Inauguration."

9. The lines quoted in *Life* magazine's coverage are from the version of the poem printed in newspapers across the United States the day after Kennedy's inauguration. These lines (and many others) are altered in subsequent printings of the poem. "The turbulence we're in the middle of / Is something we can hardly help but love" becomes, "No one of honest feeling would approve / A ruler who pretended not to love / A turbulence he had the better of." In shifting the subject of the turbulence from the people to the ruler, the revised version of the poem brings out the way in which the "ruler" (Kennedy) is seen to stand for the people, while *Life* magazine uses the lines to set the (president's) poet in the place of the people. For Frost's final version of the poem, see Stewart Udall's "Frost's 'Unique Gift Outright,'" *New York Times*, 26 Mar. 1961, as well as subsequent printings of the poem in Frost's *In the Clearing* (New York: Henry Holt and Company, 1962), 28–30, and in Edwin A. Glikes and Paul Schwaber, eds., *Of Poetry and Power: Poems Occasioned by the Presidency and by the Death of John F. Kennedy* (New York: Basic Books, 1964), 7–10.

10. Insofar as this elision is in keeping with generic American ideology, critics still sometimes miss the politics of Frost's poem. A. R. Coulthard says, for instance, "'The Gift Outright' transcends politics by catering to no party line" ("Poetry as Politics: Maya Angelou's Inaugural Poem, 'On the Pulse of Morning,'" *Notes on*

Contemporary Literature 28.1 [Jan. 1998]: 2). Coulthard launches a particularly energetic critique of both the poetics and the politics of "On the Pulse of Morning."

11. "The Gift Outright," written around 1935, was published in *A Witness Tree*
(New York: Holt and Co., 1942)—a volume that sold over ten thousand copies in
two months and won for Frost his fourth Pulitzer Prize for Poetry. The poem was
reprinted, with his dedicatory poem for Kennedy's inauguration, in *In the Clearing*
(1962), from which I quote (31).

12. Notwithstanding changes in the national discourse on multicultural-
ism that Angelou's presence on the inaugural stage signifies, for a discussion that
emphasizes the continuities between the versions of nationalism conveyed in Frost's
and Angelou's inaugural poems, see Minoo Moallem and Iain A. Boal, "Multicul-
tural Nationalism and the Poetics of Inauguration," in *Between Woman and Nation:
Nationalisms, Transnational Feminisms, and the State*, ed. Caren Kaplan, Norma
Alarcón, and Minoo Moallem (Durham, N.C.: Duke University Press, 1999),
243–63.

13. Kennedy's address at the dedication of the Robert Frost Library is included
in Glikes and Schwaber, eds., *Of Poetry and Power*, 135–37. Subsequent references
appear parenthetically in the text.

14. For a discussion of the distinction between the role of the poet in the
United States and role of the Poet Laureate in England, see William McGuire, *Poet-
ry's Catbird Seat: The Consultantship in Poetry in the English Language at the Library of
Congress, 1937–1987* (Washington, D.C.: Library of Congress, 1988), 424–32.

15. "Government and Poetry," *New York Times*, 28 Feb. 1961, 32.

16. Michael Folsom, "Poets and Presidents: Frost and Lowell," *New Orleans
Review* 5 (1979): 23.

17. See, for example, Colman McCarthy's editorial in the *Washington Post*,
19 Jan. 1993. Outside the liberal press, the tabloids, however, did their best to ruin
Angelou's character for the American people by citing the fact that she was raped as
an eight-year-old child and was an unwed mother at sixteen. And various explicitly
racist publications must have also disparaged the choice.

18. Qtd. in David Streitfeld, "The Power and the Puzzle of the Poem," *Washington Post*, 21 Jan. 1993, D11.

19. For an essay that considers the performance of the poem as integral to
its meaning, see Annette D. Sahar, Sebastian M. Benninkmeyer, and Daniel C.
O'Connell, "Maya Angelou's Inaugural Poem," *Journal of Psycholinguistic Research*
26.4 (1997): 449–63.

20. Qtd. in Streitfeld, "The Power and the Puzzle of the Poem."

21. Qtd. in Mary Schmich, "Maybe Poetry Has a Chance after All," *Chicago
Tribune*, 22 Jan. 1993, sec. 2C, p. 1.

22. Qtd. in Streitfeld, "The Power and the Puzzle of the Poem."

23. Ibid.

24. Ibid.

25. On the Random House audiotape of Angelou's "On the Pulse of Morning,"
Angelou describes the sources of the three elements in the poem as coming from
black American spirituals. Maya Angelou, *On the Pulse of Morning: The Inaugural
Poem*, audiocassette (New York: Random House Audio, 1993). Maya Angelou, "On
the Pulse of Morning," in *The Complete Collected Poems* (New York: Random House,
1994), 270–73. Subsequent references appear parenthetically in the text.

26. John Singleton, dir., *Poetic Justice: A Street Romance* (Columbia Pictures, 1993).

27. The poems spoken by Jackson come from Angelou's previously published books of poetry: "Alone" and "A Conceit" are in *Oh Pray My Wings Are Gonna Fit Me Well*; "In a Time" is in *Just Give Me a Cool Drink 'fore I Diiie*; "A Kind of Love, Some Say" and "Phenomenal Woman" are from *And Still I Rise*.

28. Justice's boss, Jesse, is also represented as an audience for her poetry. This is signaled early in the movie when she says to Justice: "You got a poem for me? Lord knows I need one."

29. Hal Hinson, "Poetic Justice," *Washington Post*, 23 July 1993. This is contrary to Angelou's own representation of the writing process: "it is not cathartic," she tells Oprah Winfrey (*Oprah Winfrey Show: One on One with Maya Angelou* [Harpo Productions, July 13, 1993]).

30. In an interview Angelou gave just before Clinton's first inauguration, Angelou makes it clear that she understands Jackson's lyrics to be "poetry."

> A: We may see, thanks to our new President, a rekindling of interest in poetry and even a rekindling in the courage to call poetry, poetry. A number of people use a form of poetry but wouldn't let it be known that they call it poetry.
> Q: For example?
> A: Young men and women who know every lyric that Michael Jackson or Janet Jackson sing. . .

Gayle Pollard Terry, "Maya Angelou: Creating a Poem to Honor the Nation," *Los Angeles Times*, 17 Jan. 1993, sec. M, p. 3.

MALIN PEREIRA

Rita Dove
Museum *and Cosmopolitanism*

Dove's view of her first volume, *The Yellow House on the Corner*, as an "apprenticeship" work demarcates her second volume, *Museum*, as her first independent aesthetic statement.[1] After presenting a cultural mulatto poetic persona (with attendant anxieties) in *Yellow House*, she confidently unfolds a fully crafted cosmopolitan aesthetic, as the echo of "muse" in the title, *Museum*, suggests.[2] Dove's comments reveal awareness of presentation in this collection: "*Museum* was very carefully thought out in terms of a book, and the impression it would make" (Rubin and Kitchen 156).

In terms of her oeuvre, the movement from "house" in the first collection to "museum" in the second underlines the implications of her enterprise. Dove begins with necessary identity construction in the house of the self and then develops a larger world construction, as implied by the museum of the world, history, and culture. As Robert McDowell notes, "The personal turning point *House on the Corner* evolves, becoming the public *Museum*" (61). In *Museum*, then, Dove builds her museum from her cosmopolitan perspective.

Museum embodies many of the key aesthetic features of the "new black aesthetic" (NBA)—one contemporary articulation of cosmopolitanism—and that is also true of Dove's earlier volume *The Yellow House on the Corner*. Both employ borrowing across race and class lines, a parodic relationship to the black arts movement, a new and unflinching look at black culture, and

---

belief in finding the universal in oneself and one's experiences (Ellis 233–51). Dove's emphasis on a worldwide range of cultures in *The Yellow House on the Corner*, the poems about the universal experiences of female adolescence, and the Don L. Lee poem critical of the black arts movement all reflect her NBA sensibility in *The Yellow House*. Her focus in that volume is elsewhere, however, and intent on constructing and publicly presenting a poetic persona in the face of some intraracial censure (chapter 3). As she has commented in interviews, the volume is very much the product of her Iowa Writer's Workshop training, an apprenticeship which, although helpful, had a stultifying effect on her poetry.

Dove took a break from writing poetry between *The Yellow House on the Corner* and *Museum*. After Iowa, she produced much of her fiction—several of the short stories collected in *Fifth Sunday* and a very early draft of her novel *Through the Ivory Gate*—as well as the first draft of her play *The Darker Face of the Earth*. She left Iowa in 1977 and moved with her husband to Oberlin, Ohio, where he taught German literature at Oberlin College for two years. They also spent three months in Ireland during that time, lived in Israel for half a year in 1979, and then moved to Germany, living there from 1979 to 1981 (personal communication from Fred Viebahn, Jan. 29, 2002). Dove focused on fiction and took frequent breaks from poetry at this point because "whenever I tried to write [a poem after Iowa], it didn't sound like me" (Peabody and Johnsen 3). After this period, she began to write the poems that became *Museum*, the first major work she considers truly her own.

Reading *Museum* as an aesthetic extension of Dove's cosmopolitanism requires unpacking two intertwined concepts, universality and personal experience, as they relate to African American literature and writers. Universality in black writing, as Marilyn Nelson Waniek observes, has become a "bugbear in Black literary criticism" (Dove and Waniek 264). These tensions have a long history that became particularly high-pitched during the 1950s and 1960s. Afro-Modernist writers of the 1950s such as Robert Hayden were attacked during the 1960s by black arts movement adherents for employing what they viewed as "white" aesthetics and cultural allusions (chapter 1). Often, the same writers and texts were simultaneously applauded by mainstream critics as attaining "universality."

Furthermore, such writers frequently maintained that their personal experiences defined them, as did any shared black group experiences. Just because those experiences were not specifically or exclusively black, however, did not mean they required purging from artistic repertoires. In his definitive literary essay on universality and personal experience, "The World and the Jug," Ralph Ellison responds to an essay by a white Jewish critic, Irving Howe, on Richard Wright, James Baldwin, and Ellison himself and attacks Howe's version of literary history in which Ellison's work can only be viewed as following (or failing to follow) Wright's legacy of the protest novel. Wright, Ellison argues, "was no spiritual father of mine" (117). Instead, he was a "relative," and other writers who influenced Ellison, regardless of race, were "ancestors": "[W]hile one can do nothing about choosing one's relatives, one can, as an artist, choose one's 'ancestors.' Wright was, in this sense, a 'relative'; Hemingway an 'ancestor.' Langston Hughes, whose work I knew in grade school and whom I knew before I knew Wright, was a 'relative'; Eliot, whom I was to meet only many years later, and Malraux and Dostoievsky and Faulkner, were 'ancestors'" (140). From this one can see how Dove's use of the word *families* in "Ö" (chapter 3) evokes such distinctions.

Ellison seems particularly irritated by Howe's limited view of black *Eigenwelt* (existential being in the world). According to Ellison, "Howe seems to see segregation as an opaque steel jug with the Negroes inside waiting for some black messiah to come along and blow the cork. . . . But if we are in a jug it is transparent, not opaque, and one is allowed not only to see outside but to read what is going on out there; to make identifications as to values and human quality" (116). The metaphor of the jug is so central to Ellison's articulation of black being in the world as it relates to African American writers and literature that it becomes his essay's title, "The World and the Jug." In the sentence I have quoted, however, he only provisionally accepts the depiction ("if") so as to make his point about black interaction with the "outer" white world.

Such a construction of the world and black existence in it—black life and culture in a jug and white life and culture outside or beyond it—constitutes a dominant spatial metaphor in perceptions of blackness in American society. (More recently, Helen Vendler's essay on Dove, "Blackness and Beyond Blackness," continues that view of black being.) Ellison's conditional acceptance of the metaphor bespeaks a more complex understanding of the ultimately decentered nature of racial and cultural interaction, an understanding beyond the scope of his argument with Howe and probably beyond the state of race relations at the time of the essay, 1963.

Ellison was working against limited views of African American identity born of a legally segregated society. One of his central arguments is that Howe's overemphasis on Wright, Baldwin, and Ellison himself as Negro writers "leaves no room for the individual writer's unique existence" (130). Ellison argues that "Howe makes of 'Negroness' a metaphysical condition," a view that "leaves no room for that intensity of personal anguish which compels the artist to seek relief by projecting it into the world in conjunction with other things; that anguish which might take the form of an acute sense of inferiority for one, homosexuality for another, an overwhelming sense of the absurdity of human life for still another" (130).[3]

According to Ellison, "The individual Negro writer must create out of his own special needs and through his own sensibilities, and these alone" (130). And that personal experience, Ellison maintains, is not only individual for a black writer but also collective by virtue of a "cultural heritage as shaped by the American experience" (131). Here Ellison uses the jug metaphor to demonstrate the largeness of the "concord of sensibilities" he finds in blacks (131): "Being a Negro American has to do with the memory of slavery and the hope of emancipation and the betrayal by allies and the revenge and contempt inflicted by our former masters after the Reconstruction, and the myths, both Northern and Southern, which are propagated in justification of that betrayal. It involves, too, a special attitude toward the waves of immigrants who have come later and passed us by. It has to do with a special perspective on the national ideals and the national conduct, and with a tragicomic attitude toward the universe" (131).

Ellison continues in this vein for another page, but his main point is that African American writers cannot, and should not, be reduced to blackness as whites might define it. They, and their writings, are shaped by individual personal experiences that also include the perspective of the shared group experience of being black. In the final line of the passage, he quietly states a black writer's capacity to comment on the universe, to be universal, through existence and perspective rather than moving beyond blackness—looking "outside the jug," so to speak.[4] That comment furnishes a key foundation.

Ellison provides a useful touchstone for Dove's deployment of key features of the new black aesthetic in *Museum*. Of the four main literary features—artists borrowing and reassembling across race and class lines; a parodic relationship to the black arts movement; a new, unflinching look at black culture, warts and all; and a belief in finding the universal in oneself and one's experiences—the first and last are most important in relation to *Museum* and other cosmopolitan works. These features, transcultural references, and a revisionist universalism reflect the cosmopolitan sensibility underlying the idea of a new black aesthetic.

Dove borrows and reassembles across race, class, and all sorts of other boundaries, a hallmark of her aesthetic from the beginning. As in *The Yellow House on the Corner*, she deliberately foregrounds her poetic identity as a poet of the world and writes from perspectives that cross history, cultures, genders, socioeconomic positions, races, and ethnicities. Many, including Robert McDowell, have noted that Dove does so; Ekaterini Georgoudaki has detailed such boundary crossings throughout Dove's four volumes of poetry, including *Museum* ("Rita Dove"). Writers of the 1950s who crossed boundaries received intraracial censure during the 1960s because they were perceived as trying to move beyond blackness and write outside the jug. Although Dove has felt similar pressures, her view of blackness and African American literature does not fit the world and the jug model that Ellison provisionally offered as a correction to Howe. Instead, Dove sees no jug of containment for black experience and being. Her wide experiences across a range of cultures have become part of the personal experience that shapes her perspective rather than being a world "out there" that she regards through a glass wall. Thus, for her, no gulf exists between the transcultural personal experiences she has had and the "concord of sensibilities" Ellison identifies as shaping a uniquely African American perspective. In discussing Derek Walcott's mixing of traditions in his use of both patois and traditional English, for example, Dove comments, "I think it's a wealth rather than a problem, and it's so ass backwards to say that there is a black way of writing and then there is a white; this is madness. Every black person that I know speaks at so many different levels all the time, and why not use all of that? All of it. Why not?" (Appendix, page 172). Dove identifies multiple language uses as a transcultural feature of black experience rather than having some be within the jug and others without.

Such a decentered, uncontained view of black being restructures universality as available to African American writers through personal experience rather than by accessing the outer, white world. This cosmopolitan belief is one of the central features of Dove's *Museum*. Dove presents a museum of the world that comes from her perspective, including personal experiences sometimes circumscribed by race (and sometimes not) as well as that "concord of sensibilities" Ellison outlines of an African American point of view. *Museum* constitutes Dove's *Harlem Gallery*, but the locus includes the world and all history as seen through Dove's perspective.[5]

This revisionist universality is typical of writers of Dove's generation. As Waniek observes, "One of the things our generation is achieving is that we are not saying, 'Look at me, I'm human too'—which is what most of the generations before us had basically been saying—but: 'Look, I'm human, and my humanity is the common denominator. Not that I have to be integrated into your humanity. My humanity is what you must find in common with *me*'" (Dove and Waniek 265).

Dove reprises Waniek's assertion in an interview with Therese Steffen. In response to the question, "What do you think about 'universalism' and the literary imagination?" Dove replies, "I don't think a universalism that lacks a sense of the specific can be very powerful; at the same time, any culturally drenched perception isn't going to be powerful if it doesn't have some kind of universal reverberation. I guess what I am saying is that 'the universal' is a bogus concept. We've come to believe that being 'universal' is to transcend difference—again, the incredible trauma of difference in modern society has made us yearn for conformity. Why can't we find the universal in those differences?" (123).

Dove's definition of the universal resembles Posnock's characterization of Du Bois's goal of negotiating "the racial particular and the unraced universal" (88), of having cultural specificity and also a sense of shared experience. Beyond that, Dove challenges any notion of obliterating difference through the universal. Instead, she values a universal focused on exploring difference. This is much the same as Michel Feher's definition of cosmopolitanism (used as part of Posnock's argument). Cosmopolitanism, Feher asserts, "entertains curiosity about . . . differences. It is 'color-curious' rather than color-blind or color-bound. . . . a cosmopolitan perspective calls for a dynamic of mutual transformation" (276).

Museum's structure makes clear that its transglobal, transcultural, transhistorical, transracial, and transgendered stances and the recurring themes of the underside of history (Rubin and Kitchen 156; Taleb-Khyar 356); the representation of artifacts; the misjudgment of beauty and ugliness; and the abuses of power spawned by cultural difference—in short, its universality—emanate from the perspective of an African American middle-class young woman. *Museum*'s four sections avoid attempting a core section like that of *The Yellow House on the Corner*. Yet Dove's arrangement of poems in sections two and three, the middle part of *Museum*, insistently marks the universal perspective of the volume as originating in the worldview of a cosmopolitan African American writer who shares sensibilities with other blacks of similar experience in America and whose point of view has been shaped by personal and familial experiences.

Museum's forty-one poems divide somewhat evenly into four sections. Section one, "The Hill Has Something to Say," contains twelve poems, although two form pairs with two others (the two on Catherine of Siena and the two involving Boccaccio and Fiammetta) thus make the section read like it has ten poems. Section two, "In the Bulrush," has ten poems; section three, "My Father's Telescope," includes nine; and section four, "Primer for the Nuclear Age," contains ten. The two poems most critical to Dove's cosmopolitan project of finding the universal in herself and her experiences (the twenty-first and twenty-second) lie directly in the middle of the volume in section two: "Agosta the Winged Man and Rasha the Black Dove" and "At the German Writers Conference in Munich."[6] These, not coincidentally, are followed by a series of personal poems involving Dove's relationship with her father (section three) and then a "universal" section (four).

In "Agosta the Winged Man and Rasha the Black Dove" (hereafter "Agosta and Rasha"), Dove inverts the objectifying gaze to which museum or cultural artifacts are exposed as she subjectifies the two German sideshow entertainers. Inversive subjectification offers details and information about those being objectified and is a key stage in creating a revisionist universalism. They become subjects who have perspectives that readers can share. That the inversion is central to the collection's enterprise as a whole is obvious not only in the central placement of the poem (twenty-one of forty-one poems) but also in the recurrence of the same inversive subjectification throughout the volume.

From the beginning of section one (the initial poem is "The Fish in the Stone"), Dove turns the tables on the objectifying gaze of history and culture. The first poem, for example, presents a fossilized fish's point of view. He is:

> weary
> of analysis, the small
> predictable truths.
> He is weary of waiting
> in the open,
> his profile stamped
> by a white light. (13)

In other poems a hill has something to say, a wife talks back to her husband, and we are invited into the stream-of-consciousness thoughts of a blues singer.

"Agosta and Rasha" represents the apex of Dove's subjectifying inversions for reasons other than the poem's central placement in the volume and Dove's choice of the painting of Agosta and Rasha as the collection's cover.[7] In the poem, which follows the process of German artist Christian Schad's composition and execution of a portrait of Agosta and Rasha in 1929, Dove offers a doubled portrait of her position as both artist and artifact. Although other poems in *Museum* also concern artists (Boccaccio, Champion Jack Dupree, and a cellist) and three present specifically African American characters, only in "Agosta and Rasha" does Dove present the issue of an artist representing a black woman. Her comments on her experience as a Fulbright scholar in Tübingen, Germany, help demonstrate how the character Rasha reflects Dove's experience. In Europe, Dove says, "I became an object. I was a Black American, and therefore I became a representative for all of that. And I sometimes felt like a ghost. I mean, people would ask me questions, but I had a feeling that they weren't seeing *me*, but a shell" (Rubin and Kitchen 156). Rasha, "so far from Madagascar" (41), parallels Dove's familiarity with feeling that she is a visual object.

The motifs of seeing and objectification by the gaze run throughout the poem.[8] Schad is depicted at the beginning as pacing his studio and then "staring" (41). Both sideshow entertainers, Agosta and Rasha, are first developed through others' visual objectifications. Dove describes Rasha's performance with a boa constrictor through Schad's recollection of the scene and how "spectators gawked." Likewise, Schad thinks of how Agosta described being observed by medical students, "his torso / exposed" (42). Schad seems concerned to distance himself from repeating these objectifying moments in the artistic representation. As he notes, "The canvas, / not his eye, was merciless." It is as if the demands of artistic representation (the canvas) might gaze mercilessly upon them but not him (his eye) (42). Ultimately, however, Rasha And Agosta invert the gaze, described by Schad in the painting as

> [w]ithout passion. Not
> the canvas
> but their gaze,
> so calm,
> was merciless. (42)[9]

The inversion of perspective and the gaze by the end of the poem is accomplished through Dove's deliberate subjectification of the two characters. She offers information and details that provide their point of view and make them subjects in the poem and thus the painting. All of that happens in Schad's mind, which suggests Dove's point. The artistic process of representation, or the cultural process of constructing history, need not objectify people into artifacts. Metaphorically speaking, we can hear what the hill has to say "if we would listen!" (19). In "Agosta and Rasha" the poet-Dove represented through Schad (who is distinct from the personal-Dove represented through Rasha) attends to the subjectivities of Agosta and Rasha. Schad recalls how Rasha, after her show (where the spectators gawked), "went back to her trailer and plucked / a chicken for dinner" (41). Later in the poem, he remembers:

> [o]nce,
> she brought fresh eggs into
> the studio, flecked and
> warm as breath. (42)

Both descriptions personalize Rasha in the process of depicting her. After being viewed as a sideshow freak, she goes home—like anyone else—and plucks a chicken for dinner. The descriptions also link Rasha to sustenance and nurturing. The eggs in particular connote fertility and life, even if cooked and eaten. Likewise, Agosta's objectification is inverted when Schad relays how Agosta, with "lip curled," spoke to him

> in wonder of women
> trailing

backstage to offer him
the consummate bloom of their lust. (42)

Such derisive amazement offers a dimension of subjectivity to Agosta that is unavailable through the medical gaze or spectators gawking.

Dove plays with the idea of taking off and putting on appearances; Agosta and Rasha are both objectified visually through physical appearance. Schad describes Rasha as moving slowly, "as if she carried / the snake around her body / always" (42). Even without the boa constrictor, she is still a snake charmer. Agosta can cover his misshapen torso, but when Schad paints him he will have "the black suit jacket / thrown off like a cloak" (42). Dove's specific mention of blackness seems a nod to the black skin color, unmentioned, that Rasha also cannot remove. The play with appearances becomes a triangle of reference among Rasha, Agosta, and Schad with Schad's reflection that

[h]e could not leave his skin—once
he'd painted himself in a new one,
silk green, worn
like a shirt. (41)

That suggests the possibility of escaping one's physical appearance (and its concomitant objectifications) through art. Dove plays with crossing boundaries of individual perspectives in this triangle of reference, suggesting that readers can do so as well by taking on various perspectives, and taking them off, via art.

Ultimately, the poem rests with the conviction that one is welded to appearance—whether skin color, physical aspects, or accessories such as snakes—and those things are inseparable from identity. Schad concludes after painting himself wearing a green shirt, "He could not leave his skin" (41); Rasha "moves slowly, as if she carried / the snake around her always" (42); and Agosta can cover but never leave

his torso
. . . its crests and fins
a colony of birds, trying
to get out. (42)

Although the imagery of "leave," "always," and "trying to get out" suggest a trapped feeling, appearances in the poem are also linked firmly to identity. The title is, after all, "Agosta the Winged Man and Rasha the Black Dove," the same title as the painting's. The two sideshow entertainers' appearances become part of their names and identities. The connection to Dove herself in Rasha's title (she is the Black Dove) further supports reading Rasha as a partial commentary on Dove's stand on blackness and identity. (That her husband Fred Viebahn's first book—seven years before he met Dove—is entitled *Die schwarzen Tauben* [The Black Doves] makes this resonate more deeply.) Dove's habit of using her last name in her poetry as a word and in bird imagery connects both Rasha the Black Dove and also Agosta the Winged Man to Dove's artistic identity as it relates to aesthetics in *Museum*.

In this poem, then, Dove as artist inverts objectified depictions of herself as a black woman (and others similarly objectified); furthermore, she returns the "merciless gaze" back on the observer. The poem's final moment, in which Agosta and Rasha look out from the canvas, states the perspective of the entire collection: Artifacts and the marginalized gaze onto both the culture and those who objectified and buried them. And Dove's gaze, or perspective, is behind it all. Thus she enacts a revisionist universalism in *Museum*.

Dove pairs this poem with the one that follows, "At the German Writers Conference in Munich," by linking imagery and theme. Unlike "Agosta and Rasha," which is experienced through Christian Schad's consciousness, the second poem uses no persona other than Dove's poet-persona; the experience presumably comes from her attendance at a conference in Munich. The perspective of the poem, then, is unabashedly Dove's, as the first stanza reveals:

> in the large hall of the Hofbräuhaus
> above the heads of the members
> of the board, taut and white
> as skin (not mine),
> tacked across a tapestry
> this banner. (43)

Dove's parenthetical denotation of her race points out the assumption of "universal" acceptance of white when no markers are given to denote other skin colors. The words "not mine" are slipped in as if they are a minor aside, but in reality they turn the perspective of the entire poem, just as in "Agosta and Rasha." The image of skin, of course, also ties back to the preceding poem and is a reminder that skin color (and other facts of physical appearance) is interwoven with identity. Thus the perspective of the volume is again underlined as being that of a black woman.

The poem sounds Dove's theme of repression of aspects of history, with the focal point being a medieval tapestry partially covered by a large white paper banner that states the organizing group of the conference. The banner obscures most of the tapestry, yet the "tapestry pokes out / all over," expressing the eruptions of repressed history (43). The substance of the poem details reading the tapestry's parts, which represent history outside a frame. Dove's parenthetical insertion of her skin color "(not mine)" acts as a similar eruption of history and culture in the text of *Museum* (43). As such, it becomes a central statement of aesthetic perspective that refuses to "paper over" a false presentation of skin color as "universally" white. At this moment in the text, Dove asserts a universally relevant vantage point that comes from an African American perspective.

After the two central poems in *Museum*, Dove's new black aesthetic of finding the universal in oneself and one's experiences finds expression in the structural interplay between the last two sections. The third section, "My Father's Telescope," concerns the poet's father and their relationship. The fourth section, "Primer for the Nuclear Age," ranges across the globe and throughout the contemporary era. As Dove explains some of the connections between the two sections:

> The entire third section deals with my father. . . . I was trying to look into the fourth section with the telescope so that it becomes much more; it becomes the technological age, the scientific age, the nuclear age, that I'm looking forward to. . . .
> Rubin: And finally you have the "Primer for the Nuclear Age," which extends the theme, as you said, to everything.
> Dove: Yes, looking outward again after going to the father. I also didn't want the father poems to appear too early in the book. . . . But after two sections where there's nothing personal at all, I wanted to go into the personal poems and then explode out of them into the nuclear age. And I do believe that the kinds of events which are formed by the cruelty of Trujillo or the carelessness of nuclear escalation nowadays start at very personal levels. (Rubin and Kitchen 159)

Dove here confirms that, for her, the personal undergirds the global. Thus in section four her move to the global or "universal" comes only after, and is fundamentally informed by, her individual perspective as reinforced by section three. She makes this structural interplay apparent in the poem "Anti-Father" in section three, in which she speaks back to a father—both her personal father and also the father of "universal law"—and asserts,

> [c]ontrary to
> tales you told us
> . . . .

—the stars
are not far
apart. Rather
they draw
closer together
with years. (54)

"[W]oman to man," she tells him, "outer space is / inconceivably / intimate" (55).

Dove's revision of the universe—and the universal—from her perspective (in this poem specifically female) helps readers understand "Parsley," the final poem of section four and the volume, as also informed by her individual perspective. Rafael Trujillo, the Dominican dictator who is said to have had twenty thousand Haitian canefield workers killed because they could not pronounce the word *parsley* (*perejil*) in Spanish, represents great evil to Dove because he refuses to appreciate difference (78).[10] Instead, Trujillo kills because of a repressive universalism that enforces the dominant party's culture and experience over those of others. As the workers note, in El General's version of universalism, "He is all the world / there is" (75). Because his mother "could roll an R like a queen," such linguistic ability should be a standard of humanity, and Trujillo will kill to enforce it. Dove condemns such oppressive universalism and contrasts it with revisionist universalism such as her own, which depicts subjects enacting a dynamic of mutual transformation because of cosmopolitan curiosity about difference.

* * *

Several among Dove's contemporaries in African American poetry could be named as cosmopolitan, among them Yusef Komunyakaa, Toi Derricotte, and Cyrus Cassells. Of the younger generation, Elizabeth Alexander, who studied with Derek Walcott, could also be identified. To what extent they might also consider themselves part of any new black aesthetic is debatable. Komunyakaa, for example, might agree to being cosmopolitan but would certainly insist that his work is founded on a blues and jazz aesthetic.[11]

Other aesthetics were also evident in African American poetry during the 1980s and 1990s. Cheryl Clarke, for example, in *Living as a Lesbian*, writes in a deliberate refusal of traditional aesthetic poetic values, as Melissa Daniel notes. Brenda Marie Osbey's work offers a New Orleans-specific narrative poetic that eschews the figurative.[12] And Wanda Coleman's blunt, energetic poetry attacks the evils of racism, sexism, and classism in a style insistently oral and polemical. Furthermore, a new generation's interest in performance or "spoken-word" poetry, which has connections to hip-hop culture, is another dominant poetic aesthetic; individual wordsmiths now appear on CDs and in published anthologies (Anglesey; Wannberg).[13]

Cosmopolitanism is assuming a centrally important role in academic circles for several reasons, especially class differences. Ellis notes the vastly expanded black middle class as a factor behind the black arts of the 1980s. As the twentieth century came to a close, fully 50 percent of the black American population was middle class or above. With such economic advancement came an array of educational and cultural experiences and a concomitant entrance into institutional positions of power.

African American cosmopolitan poets come from graduate programs such as those at the University of Iowa, Brown University, and New York University and have bachelor's degrees from institutions such as Stanford, Wesleyan, and Yale universities. They tend to have traveled extensively and have lived abroad for extended periods, for example, in Germany, France, Senegal, Italy, and Vietnam. They have academic appointments, often at prestigious universities such as Columbia University, the University of Virginia, and the University of Chicago. They also are generally well published, having found acceptance in key venues such as the *American Poetry Review, New England Review, Bread Loaf Quarterly*, and the *Kenyon Review* as well as the preeminent journal for African American literary arts and criticism, *Callaloo*. Their books appear with major publishers such as Norton and Random House as well as with well-respected poetry presses such as Copper Canyon, the University of Virginia's *Callaloo* Poetry Series, and Wesleyan University Press. They also have been successful at winning grants, fellowships, awards, and residencies to support their work from institutions such as the Ford Foundation, the National Endowment for the Arts, the Academy of American Poets, the Rockefeller Foundation, the Lannan Foundation, the National Humanities Center, and the Fulbright, Guggenheim and Mellon Fellowships. Both Yusef Komunyakaa and Rita Dove have won Pulitzer Prizes for Poetry.

Thus, in terms of institutional sanction by African American, American, and international culture brokers, cosmopolitan poets are prominent in the generation of African American poets who were born after 1940 and published throughout the 1980s and 1990s. Although Wanda Coleman has complained that she could not find enough money to bury her son and that she has been shunned in African American poetry circles, cosmopolitan poets are generally well funded and well fêted, indicating their high stature since the 1980s.[14] When the George Moses Horton Society for the Study of African American Poetry (founded by Trudier Harris-Lopez of the University of North Carolina at Chapel Hill) held its inaugural conference in 1998, for example, the three poets of focus included one "elder" in the tradition,

Margaret Walker, and two cosmopolitan poets, Komunyakaa and Dove. In addition, when the Academy of American Poets finally relented in the face of overwhelming criticism of their all-white chancellors' group (thanks to an aggressive campaign by Fred Viebahn following a written complaint by Toi Derricotte), they appointed Komunyakaa a chancellor along with Lucille Clifton, whose work is more representative of the previous generation. Dove has received a high degree of public attention in her two-term appointment as poet laureate and her authorship of the "Poet's Choice" column (begun by Robert Hass) in *Book World*. If we agree with Michel Feher and Ross Posnock, who argue that cosmopolitanism has been repressed in the black intellectual tradition, it is apparent that the 1980s and 1990s represented a two-decade emergence into prominence.

It is worth reflecting on the politics of this academic prominence. If 50 percent of black America is middle-class or above, then the other half is not (Raymond). Henry Louis Gates, Jr., and Cornel West have identified the bifurcation in African American culture as a key issue for the twenty-first century, a continuation and redefinition of Du Bois's articulation in 1903 that the problem of the twentieth century is the problem of the color line. The problem of the twenty-first century appears to be the class line within the community. Gates comments that "Dr. King did not die so that *half* of us would 'make it,' and *half* of us perish" (xvii, emphasis in the original).

Spoken-word poetry, with its connection to hip-hop popular culture, often urban and overtly political themes, and frequent protest of racial and class oppression, is the aesthetic vehicle for those outside the black middle class. The aesthetic itself is slowly gaining academic and institutional recognition by teachers, scholars, and established poetry organizations. It appears prominent in popular culture—more students know it than know the work of Rita Dove. The prominence of cosmopolitanism in academic culture thus may be born of privilege and the class schism in African American literature. In general, the youngest poets who garnered academic attention during the 1990s—Elizabeth Alexander, Melvin Dixon, and the Dark Room Collective—all seem to be from the half that "made it." Poets such as Angela Jackson, who is committed to the people of Chicago's South Side, are almost completely unknown. When including more popular poetry in our sights, cosmopolitanism seems only one of several current threads in African American literature; that encourages scholars and institutions to broaden their understanding.

Notes

1. In an interview with William Walsh, Dove remarked that *Yellow House*, "like many first books is a hodgepodge of techniques and visions. . . . 'Ö' [the last

poem of that volume] felt like a very different poem, one that signaled the end of an apprenticeship" (150).

2. Thanks to Ilona Cesan for this insight.

3. One cannot help but wonder if Ellison intended these three specific cases to correspond to Wright, Baldwin, and Ellison directly.

4. Ross Posnock's take on the problem with universalism is white refusal to acknowledge black contributions to the larger culture (20). From that perspective, the universal is composed of everyone; it is only the fiction of cultural segregation, perpetuated in the interests of white dominance, that makes people believe otherwise.

5. Although Dove has pointed in interviews to the German *Mausoleum* by Hans Magnus Enzensberger as an inspiration for *Museum*, it seems likely that a model or influence closer to home is Tolson's *Harlem Gallery*, especially given Dove's essay on it within two years of *Museum*'s publication (Peabody and Johnsen; Taleb-Khyar).

6. Robert McDowell also pairs these two poems (65).

7. It is also notable that Dove, in this early poem, deliberately suppresses her apprehensions about an attack from black arts movement adherents (Steffen, "The Darker Face" 108).

8. Although I have in mind some of the ideas about the male objectifying gaze first promulgated by Laura Mulvey and later the subject of some degree of feminist theorizing, I am not directly drawing on the gender implications here as much as the mechanism of visual objectification.

9. McDowell notes the shift of their gaze outward at the end of the poem (65).

10. Fred Viebahn notes the correct date of this mass murder is 1937 rather than 1957 as originally footnoted in *Museum* (personal communication. Jan. 29, 2002). Historians offer differing interpretations of the causes behind the massacre. Robert Crassweller, for example, posits that Trujillo, who had been plotting to overthrow Haiti, ordered the massacre in retaliation for the killing of his underground agents in Haiti. Crassweller perceives no "general prejudice" or "color prejudice" toward Haitians on the part of Dominicans (149).

In contrast, Eric Roorda argues that the "Dominican nationalism promoted by Trujillo emphasized Hispanic culture and demonized Haitian, African-derived culture" (129). Trujillo's attempts to reduce Haitian influence and border-crossings were revealed to him as unsuccessful during a tour of the border in August and September 1937 (130–31). On October 2, 1937, he announced his intent to permanently eliminate the Haitian presence in the Dominican Republic (131). Although Crassweller mentions the pronunciation of *perejil* as a test (155), neither historian considers it a cause of the massacre.

11. Thanks to Craig Werner for helping me articulate this distinction.

12. See Lynn Keller's balanced and informative study of Osbey in *Forms of Expansion*.

13. Thanks to Veronica Jones, a spoken-word poet herself, for introducing me to the next generation.

14. Wanda Coleman's letters to E. Ethelbert Miller appear in *Callaloo*.

ANGELA M. SALAS

Human Empathy and Negative Capability: Yusef Komunyakaa's Poetry

I left America because I doubted my ability to survive the fury of the color problem here. . . . I wanted to prevent myself from becoming *merely* a Negro; or even, merely a Negro writer. I wanted to find out in what way the *specialness* of my experience could be made to connect me with other people instead of dividing me from them.

—James Baldwin, *Nobody Knows My Name*

Racial recusal is a forlorn hope. In a system where whiteness is the default, racelessness is never a possibility. You cannot opt out. You can only opt in.

—Henry Louis Gates, Jr., "The Passing of Anatole Broyard"

The epigraphs above illustrate a tension that must still be felt by many artists as we begin the twenty-first century. James Baldwin writes of his need to get away from the United States to keep from "becoming *merely* a Negro; or even, merely a Negro writer." Baldwin needed to escape the omnipresence of his color and what it has meant in this country to become a writer who could connect with readers, rather than speaking to them from across a yawning racial chasm. Whether Baldwin found it more necessary to escape other people's constructions of his race, or his own, internalized, constructions is a subject for speculation, but not, I think, one for which we will ever find an answer.

If we read Baldwin's haunting lament against the ideals of Pablo Neruda, who calls poetry "a deep inner calling in man," and who confers upon poets a sacred duty to enter the priesthood of letters and "interpret the light,"[1] we see a disheartening gap between Neruda's ideal and the reality of Baldwin's troubled life. Neruda would have poets be the acknowledged legislators of the world; in contrast, Baldwin's career was one of protracted, painful negotiation with that world. Refusal to negotiate as Baldwin needed to may explain, in part, writer Anatole Broyard's decision to pass as white. As Henry Louis Gates, Jr. notes in his essay about Broyard, that author "did not want to write about black love, black passion, black suffering, black joy; he wanted to write about love and passion and suffering and joy. We give lip service to the idea of the writer who happens to be black, but had anyone, in the postwar era, ever seen such a thing?"[2] Would readers have recognized such an author if they *had* seen one, or would they, African American and white, have accused the author of ducking the artists' responsibilities to *engage* with race, and of being a dark imitator of the European masters?

Meditating on Broyard's "choice" and Gates's essay about it, critic Susan Gubar writes that Broyard's "racial imposture . . . hints that whiteness remains 'the default position' for individuality, whereas blackness continues to be attached to the concept of race, of race type, and thus to race prejudice."[3] One consequence of this "default position" of whiteness is the literary ghetto of which the cosmopolitan poet Robert Hayden wrote in 1967, when he suggested that the critical tendency to see established African American authors as spokespeople for their race placed "any Negro author in a kind of literary ghetto where the standards applied to other writers are not likely to be applied to him."[4] In short, race may trump all else in far too many readers' relationship to the works of writers of color. These readers may see poetry or fiction as imaginative bits of sociology or political theory, the subjects of which are assumed to be determined by their author's color. The canonical greats, it is suggested, wrote and read from a position of *universal* humanity; however, nonwhite writers are perceived as *special*, hence bracketed, in ways such authors as William Shakespeare and William Blake are not.

One can make a convincing case that many fine authors have contended with the backhanded compliment of being read and described as spokespeople for their race, their gender, or those sharing their sexual identity, rather than as individual craftspeople whose subjectivity was and is informed, but not determined, by the thing that makes their vision singular. Whether reading about German history, Greek mythology, homosexuality, or the burdens of parenthood, many readers still seek a convenient monolithic "African

American" perspective from African American authors. It is precisely this expectation and the "literary ghetto" it creates that made Baldwin despair and Broyard deny both his heritage and his family.

What is a writer to do when she or he seeks to "interpret the light" for many readers, but is chided that all humans are locked in the prisonhouses of our own subjectivity; that our *specialness*, to return again to Baldwin's words, does, in fact, divide us from others? Are we all, readers and writers, "serial hyphenates," speaking from different unconnectable subject positions? Can an author function from various hyphenate positions in turn and thus pull together a vision of the world that foregrounds his or her common humanity, as well as the humanity of the people reading that author's work? Further, can a writer reeducate readers who assume that whiteness is "'the default position' for individuality"?

I have no sure answers for any of these questions, although I frequently find myself chasing their chimera. In order to harness these ideas, however, I intend in this chapter to trace the conflict between Neruda's priesthood and Baldwin's ghetto as it arises in Yusef Komunyakaa's career. Komunyakaa, born in 1947, is arguably one of the most respected, influential, and anthologized poets of his generation. He institutionalizes his aesthetic beliefs when serving as a juror for poetry contests, a mentor for writers, and as the eloquent subject of numerous published interviews. Thus Komunyakaa's determined arc towards an all-encompassing vision, with his simultaneous and stubborn honoring of the particularity of the sources of his vision, may be instructive to readers who are invested in answers to the questions raised above.

Yusef Komunyakaa's literary career reveals a specific aesthetic attempt to achieve an unmediated connection with his readers: a connection informed, but not determined, by his life and experiences as an African American man. These attempts are in some way akin to those of James Baldwin. As a teenager, Komunyakaa read Baldwin's *Nobody Knows My Name* (from which the first epigraph was taken) in the segregated public library of his home town of Bogalusa, Louisiana; he has cited Baldwin's work as instrumental in the formation of his consciousness.[5] Komunyakaa has traveled widely, to such places as Mexico, Vietnam, Japan, and Australia; it is notable, however, that he has not needed to become an expatriate, as did Baldwin, to become a successful writer. Perhaps Baldwin's account of his own dilemmas gave Komunyakaa the mental space to map out his human journey; more likely, the phenomenal, if uncompleted, changes in the social and racial status quo in the United States have given the younger writer an emotional and psychological liberation Baldwin lacked.[6]

While drawing strength from the particularity of his experience as an African American and a Southerner, and as a veteran of the American war in

Vietnam, Komunyakaa nonetheless insists that he can function imaginatively from many different positions, not all of which derive from autobiography. In his career, Komunyakaa has taken on the personae of many people, including a female Vietnamese rape victim, tricksters, a white member of a lynch mob, combat veterans, and his remembered childhood self, a feat he accomplishes in *Magic City* (1992). Indeed, Komunyakaa maintains that that a poet must have a capacity for human empathy, saying that "the world is so large, and we are so small. How dare an artist *not* imagine the world from the perspective of someone other than himself? It's all part of the ongoing dialogue we must have between ourselves and the world."[7] Race, gender, age, experience, and upbringing inform our perceptions of the world, but they needn't contain our imaginations and sympathies. Thus, while sternly rendering racial intimidation in the Jim Crow South in "History Lessons," from *Magic City*, Komunyakaa also imagines the dreams of Vietnamese refugees, in *Dien Cai Dau's* "Boat People" (1988). Komunyakaa enlarges our imaginations to encompass both a frightened grandmother whispering "*Son, you ain't gonna live long*" to the youth who faces down a bullying white deliveryman, and the Vietnamese refugees who "cling to each other, / faces like yellow sea grapes, / wounded by doubt & salt."

While Komunyakaa's attempts to imagine the world from other perspectives have sometimes been audacious, as in the poems "You and I Are Disappearing" and "Re-creating the Scene," in *Dien Cai Dau*, they have also evolved over the course of his career. Since the publication of *I Apologize for the Eyes in My Head* (1986), Komunyakaa has moved from singular racial and gender identities, to still more imaginative "hyphenated" positions rooted in his own experiences, to a projected identity that seeks to erase the specificity of the narrator and, as importantly, the reader.[8] The first lines of the first poem in *I Apologize* are a rebuke to "Introduce me first as a man. / Don't mention superficial laurels / the dead heap up on the living. / I am a man." The enumeration of the things the speaker is and *is* and is *not* gestures to his identity, beyond the confines of his race. Indeed, the poem continues, asserting, in lines 11 through 21:

> I am a man. I've scuffled
> in mudholes, broken teeth in a grinning skull
> like the moon behind bars. I've done it all
> to be known as myself. No titles.
> I have principles. I won't speak
> on the natural state of the unicorn
> in literature or self-analysis.
> I have no birthright to prove,

no insignia, no secret
password, no fleur-de-lis.
My initials aren't on a branding iron.[9]

In short, the speaker's life and his actions have moved him outside the trivial sorts of labeling devices with which people limit themselves, or are limited by others. You cannot call me "X" the speaker asserts, because that name does not take into account the things I have done and experienced—things that are beyond the rigid signifiers you might wish to apply to me. Importantly, the narrator's humanity is tied to his *masculinity*, evidenced by his demand to be introduced as a *man*; he will allow neither his masculinity nor his humanity to be called into question. This suggests that at the time Komunyakaa wrote this piece, which opens his first widely reviewed volume of poetry, he was still learning to render experience beyond the signifiers of gender, despite being quite clear-eyed about the problems presented by racial signifiers. His narrator seeks to transcend race, yet frames his disclaimer in terms of masculine prowess, asserting that he has "scuffled / in mudholes, broken teeth in a grinning skull / like the moon behind bars." In this poem, Komunyakaa invokes a long-standing tradition in African American literary and civic life by framing his antiracist critique with the assertion "I am a man." Clearly, Komunyakaa is not seeking to deny or diminish the fact of his dark skin and all that such skin means in the United States; he is, rather, asserting himself beyond the generic signifiers of "person" or "human being," signifiers which, as Susan Gubar suggests, actually imply *whiteness* as the universal human condition.

The poem ends "Inside my skin, / loving you, I am this space / my body believes in," suggesting an attempt on the poet's part to claim his body and everything that comes with it as his own—to wrest his black, male body away from the gaze of a world preoccupied with the bodies of black men, whether as aesthetic and sexual objects or as the objects of fear and mistrust.[10] Being a *man* and possessing a male body are not necessarily the same thing; thus, Komunyakaa's narrator claims himself as a space his "body believes in." In short, his boundaries, and the boundaries of the love of which he speaks in the final lines of the poem, are not fixed by corporeal barriers. The poet is more than the experiences of which he writes, although it is these experiences ("I've done it all / to be known as myself") that contribute to his status as *a man*. It may be that Komunyakaa himself needed to celebrate his masculinity and assert the privileges that come with it before he could undertake the task of rendering the subjectivities of others; each volume since *I Apologize for the Eyes in My Head* has evidenced increasingly bold attempts to encompass the world in all its complexity. Indeed, while Komunyakaa's narrators are never "raceless" and never fall into the "default position" of implied whiteness, their observations are not bounded by their race. They are, rather, enriched by it.[11]

When Komunyakaa published *Dien Cai Dau*, a volume addressing the experiences and observations of an African American serviceman during the Vietnam War, he was beginning to immerse himself in the experiences of people whose lives were different from his own. "Re-creating the Scene" is one example of a poem in which Komunyakaa began a strikingly active imaginative engagement with the perspectives of other people. In "Re-creating the Scene," discussed more fully in chapter 3, Komunyakaa imagines the scene of a Vietnamese woman's rape and subsequent murder by American soldiers. The juxtaposition of a protective mother as a frail "torn water flower" and her rapists as "gods" inside their tank, where they take turns "piling stones / on her father's grave" (defiling both her body and her family name) is startling and apt. While these U.S. soldiers may be the victims of a racist and classist nation, they do untold, irreparable damage to those who are smaller and weaker than they are; they shore up their own wounded self-regard through sexual assault. Komunyakaa suggests to readers that these soldiers may be sinned against, may be small and vulnerable as combatants in a frightening foreign land, but that they also sin—and terribly.

Throughout "Re-creating the Scene," Komunyakaa simultaneously attempts to render the experience of a person not often seen in American literature, while suggesting the ultimate impossibility of truly "knowing" this experience. The poem rejects any impulse to tidy, or to corral its meanings for readers; thus, it is an unsettling poem, and one that manifests Komunyakaa's decision to transcend the particularity of the experience he offered in "Unnatural State of the Unicorn." "Recreating the Scene" is not a mea culpa, as the narrator has had nothing to do with this crime, and it is not an apologia for the soldiers (on the order of "pity these poor young men, made into brutes and rapists by the horrors of the war in Vietnam"). Rather, the poem is an arresting look at the sordidness of the rape ("the three men / ride her breath, grunting / over lovers back in Mississippi") and how useless the rules against war crimes are to a female civilian. It is a basic human right that one not be raped, and a basic legal right to seek redress should this right be transgressed; however, should the woman attempt to claim her rights, she is likely to be killed, or to endanger the rest of her family. The rules do not matter, and the laws do not protect her.

It is notable that Komunyakaa's narrator, a military journalist, remains outside of these events, never claiming to understand anything, from the motivations of the soldiers to the ultimate fate of their victim. The details he lays, one by one, are all conjecture, as the poem's title makes clear. Still, it is a powerful, wrenching poem, and the fact that the narrator *must* recreate the scene in the victim's absence adds to, rather than detracts from, its power. One wonders about this woman, and about her child, who "grabs the air, / searching for a breast" and one gets no answer, except for a certain, sinking feeling that both are the long dead victims of what we in the United States still attempt to see as a noble cause undertaken by fine young men and a highly principled United States government.

Another stunning poem from *Dien Cai Dau* is "You and I Are Disappearing," which was subsequently included in Elliot Goldenthal's *Fire, Paper, Water: A Vietnam Oratorio* (1996). The poem describes the death of a Vietnamese woman by napalm, and in it Komunyakaa's narrator is like a piece of film, marked forever by what it has captured and been captured by. "You and I Are Disappearing" is an account of an experience that the narrator must remember again and again, despite the anguish such remembering causes him. It begins with the haunting assertion that "The cry I bring down from the hills / belongs to a girl still burning / inside my head." Komunyakaa piles simile upon simile to describe the woman's death; such a device places the reader apart from, yet witness to, the woman's horrifying death. In Komunyakaa's narrative, she burns

> like a sack of dry ice.
> She burns like oil on water.
> She burns like a cattail torch
> dipped in gasoline.
> She glows like the fat tip
> of a banker's cigar,
>   silent as quicksilver. . . .
> She burns like a field of poppies
> at the edge of a rain forest . . .
> . . . .
> She burns like a burning bush
> driven by a godawful wind.[12]

It is as though mere words, words absent of symbol and simile, will never be enough to truly show the violent catastrophe of death by napalm. The propulsive layering of similes upon each other suggests, indeed creates, a certain narrative frenzy. If the victim is rendered not-human, it is because of the napalm, not because Komunyakaa lacks the imagination to do her justice. Indeed, Komunyakaa elevates the ever-dying woman to biblical status when he finally describes her as burning "like a burning bush / driven by a godawful wind." These lines remind us of God made manifest in the burning bush of the book of Exodus, but they also empty that allusion of its hopeful promise of liberation. Moses received instruction and guidance from the burning bush; the horror of this woman's death simply replays itself, ad infinitum, in the appalled narrator's mind.

"You and I Are Disappearing" is a haunting poem, turned into a frightening lament by Elliot Goldenthal's score for *Fire, Water, Paper*. The narrator attests to having been a witness to this death (the poem opens with the lines "The cry I bring down from the hills / belongs to a girl still burning / inside my head") and he attempts to find the words to match this horrible spectacle. The choices Komunyakaa makes, and the similes he uses, speak to the trauma that the sight has inflicted upon the speaker; however, this narrator does not make himself the central character in the poem. This is not a poem about how terrible it was for the narrator to witness a civilian's horrible death. What matters in the poem is the dying "girl," the fact that she is Vietnamese, and that she is immolated by a chemical manufactured to permit Americans to kill from a safe distance. It is the woman's suffering, not the narrator's, which Komunyakaa reanimates for readers. In "You and I Are Disappearing" Komunyakaa writes as a Jeremiah rather than a journalist, reminding readers of the human cost of the Vietnam War, a cost inscribed on Vietnamese bodies as well as on American ones.

One of the triumphs of "You and I Are Disappearing" is that Komunyakaa turns an abstract "victim" or "enemy" into a suffering person. He offers readers a chance to see beyond and through postwar clichés to the humanity of a suffering person, a "girl" destroyed by war, by reaching through tired imagery and showing the agony of death by napalm, an agony only a highly attuned imagination could render to such effect. The poem itself brings to mind the refrain from William Butler Yeats's poem "Easter 1916": "A terrible beauty is born." "Terrible beauty" is a poignant paradox, and the image of a person burning "like a field of poppies / at the edge of a rain forest" is terribly, and dreadfully, beautiful.

Magic City (1992) reanimates Komunyakaa's childhood home of Bogalusa, Louisiana. Bogalusa was known as Magic City to the Choctaw who had once inhabited the land upon which the town was founded. The volume is marked by the time and place Komunyakaa reflects upon: the pre–Civil Rights, Jim Crow South. As such, it is an extended meditation upon race, class, and gender and how these things mark—indeed, vex—the lives of those with whom Komunyakaa grew up. In poems such as "Glory," readers can feel immediacy, and a resonance, in the experience Komunyakaa outlines:

Most were married teenagers
Working knockout shifts daybreak
To sunset six days a week—

Already old men playing ball
In a field between a row of shotgun houses
& the Magazine Lumber Company.
They were all Jackie Robinson
& Willie Mays, a touch of
Josh Gibson & Satchell Paige
in each stance and swing, a promise
Like a hesitation pitch always
At the edge of their lives,
Arms sharp as rifles.
The Sunday afternoon heat
Flared like thin flowered skirts
As children & wives cheered.
The men were like cats
Running backwards to snag
Pop-ups & high-flies off
Fences, stealing each other's glory.
The old deacons & raconteurs
Who umpired made an *Out* or *Safe*
Into a song & dance routine.
Runners hit the dirt
& slid into homeplate,
Cleats catching light,
As they conjured escapes, outfoxing
Double plays. In the few seconds
It took a man to eye a woman
Upon the makeshift bleachers,
A stolen base or homerun
Would help another man
Survive the new week.[13]

The baseball game is necessary play, much like the wood-splitting scene in Robert Frost's "Two Tramps at Mudtime" ("Only where love and need are one / and the work is play for mortal stakes / is the deed ever really done / for heaven and the future's sake"). The makeshift field is a field of dreams, where teenage fathers are heroes to their wives and children. It's more than just a game as players "hit the dirt"—a singularly military phrase—to slide into home plate. The play is precise but animated, and it arrests the attention of family members and neighbors. These young men "already old" are men readers may recognize, whether by having been raised by such men—heroes on the weekend, mere underpaid "labor" during the work week—or through popular constructions of such men. "Glory" is as apt a commentary on class and on limiting concepts of masculinity as it is upon race; as such, it deftly conveys the pathos of the young working-class players' social and economic limitations. In the essay "True Confessions" in Thelma Golden's volume *Black Male: Representations of Masculinity in Contemporary American Art*, Kobena Mercer and Isaac Julien remind us that "social definitions of what it is to be a man, about what constitutes 'manliness,' are not 'natural' but are historically constructed and this construction is culturally variable. . . . [B]lack male gender identities have been culturally constructed through complex dialectics of power."[14] Indeed, the small but important consolations of this baseball game show how circumscribed the concept of "manhood" is for these young men.

"Man" as athlete and breadwinner suggests "not-man" or "unmanned" if one is neither an athlete nor financially secure. What happens to the working-class African American men of "Glory," already underpaid and overworked, thus only marginally "men" on the economic scale, if they are injured, or if they become too old to play well? When a poem of such kinetic grace ends with the lines "a stolen base or homerun / would help another man / survive the new week," we know that these graceful weekend athletes, like their families, are trapped by poverty, obligation, and dead-end jobs in dead-end towns with ironic nicknames such as Magic City. There will come a day when they cannot play—or when their families will stop wanting to see them do so. When that day comes, these men will need something else to help them "survive the new week." That something else might be despair, alcohol, drugs, infidelity, domestic abandonment, or the abuse of those who no longer idealize him. Whatever it is, the substitute is unlikely to be a true consolation for a life's promise spent earning poor wages for hard work, and for seeing one's potential recede "like a hesitation pitch" from the edges of one's life.

Later in *Magic City* Komunyakaa fast-forwards to one such young man's future. The oft-reprinted "My Father's Loveletters" give readers a glimpse of what happens when men and women see their life's possibilities foreclosed upon. Komunyakaa is notable for the balance with which he treats a father who has splintered his family and has grown to understand that he cannot undo the damage he has wrought:

> On Fridays he'd open a can of Jax
> After coming home from the mill,
> & ask me to write a letter to my mother
> Who sent postcards of desert flowers
> Taller than men. He would beg,
> Promising never to beat her

Again. Somehow I was happy
She had gone, & sometimes wanted
To slip in a reminder, how Mary Lou
Williams' "Polka Dots & Moonbeams"
Never made the swelling go down.
His carpenter's apron always bulged
With old nails, a claw hammer
Looped at his side & extension cords
Coiled at his feet.
Words rolled from under the pressure
Of my ballpoint: Love,
Baby, Honey, Please.
We sat in the quiet brutality
Of voltage meters & pipe threaders,
Lost between sentences . . .
The gleam of a five-pound wedge
On the concrete floor
Pulled a sunset
Through the door of his toolshed.
I wondered if she laughed
& held them over the gas burner.
My father could only sign
His name, but he'd look at blueprints
& say how many bricks
Formed each wall. This man,
Who stole roses & hyacinth
For his yard, would stand there
With his eyes closed & fists balled,
Laboring over a simple word, almost
Redeemed by what he tried to say.[15]

The father is a man of action, uncomfortable with words. Thus, clichés of "Love / Baby, Honey, Please" express his most sincere feelings of regret and loneliness—and these words come out laboriously, with the aid of beer. He is kin to the parent in Robert Hayden's "Those Winter Sundays." The silent father of Hayden's poem, having accepted "love's austere and lonely offices," arises before everyone else and makes "banked fires blaze," a gift for which he is not thanked, at least in part because "the chronic angers" of the household obscure his acts of service. For his part, the father of Komunyakaa's poem returns from a hard day's work, then labors over his love letters, virtually inarticulate despite the clear sincerity of his regret and his desire to begin again with the woman who has left him in a search for happiness and safety.

While the "chronic angers" of Hayden's adolescent household are never explained in "Those Winter Sundays," Komunyakaa spares us little in suggesting why his narrator's mother has left her family. In his epistles, her husband "would beg / Promising never to beat her / Again." The narrator follows that stark word "again" with the memory of being happy that his mother is gone and wanting to "slip in a reminder" about his father's violence, lest love or loyalty lead her back to a prison of fear and humiliation. The son may be proud of his father's ability to read the blueprint for a wall, and he may admire that man's ability to make things grow, but he knows from experience that his father has been an angry, brutal man.

Komunyakaa's narrator, looking back upon his childhood, pronounces his father complex and gifted, even tender, but asserts that he is not redeemed from the harm he has caused his wife and family. His father's words, no matter how hard they come, or how earnestly they are meant, cannot make "the swelling go down" or cause the painful memories his family harbors to disappear. Still, Komunyakaa has given a portrait of this father's humanity; he has driven his wife away, but he also dutifully goes to work and provides for his remaining family. Frustration and a warped sense of his male prerogatives led him to abuse his wife; however, adult responsibility and honor keep him providing for the children who have witnessed and perhaps been the recipients of the rage that has fractured his marriage. Redeemed this father may not be; nor, in Komunyakaa's poem, is he damned for what he has done.

Childhood may be a rich source of creative tension, but writing about one's childhood can be dangerous to an aspiring author. It is hard to be objective about one's childhood, and if one cannot be objective—if one is simply kicking against old injustices and the way they made one feel—then one's work is unlikely to be interesting or artful. There is certainly an audience for confessional poetry about the ravages of life as a misunderstood or frightened child, but this audience is often looking for titillating disclosure, caring little about the literary quality inhering in such revelations. As such, the work may be therapy for writer and reader rather than art. Louise Gluck once observed about a volume of poetry that did not, in her estimation, hold together *as* poems, that "the true object of love (in the book) is the suffering child, and the problem for artists dealing with this material is not to write from pity for the child one was but to devise a language or point of view that reinhabits anguish."[16]

One source of the power of "My Father's Loveletters" is that Komunyakaa devises "a language or point of view that reinhabits anguish." The narrator is his father's scribe, a boy who grows to become an author who breathes life into these moments of his family's history. As with "Re-creating the Scene" and "You And I Are Disappearing," "My Father's Loveletters" is not about the narrator's anguish. It is not centrally concerned with the pain the narrator may or may not carry with him as a result of his parents' disastrous marriage. There is no meditation about how the narrator's childhood witnessing of domestic violence has shaped his attitudes towards, or relationships with, women. Rather, the piece is so careful and restrained ("We sat in the quiet brutality / Of voltage meters & pipe threaders, / Lost between sentences . . .") and the narrative is so precise that the piece is more forceful than it might had Komunyakaa written a brutal, angry poem. The image of a child who "sometimes" wants to remind his mother that she's safer away from her husband—but doesn't do so—is poignant. What restrains the son from adding such a note of warning? Surely he does not fear that his unlettered father will be able to read the note. Perhaps this young Cyrano is already practicing the poet's art of observation without interference. In any case, Komunyakaa's narrator is able to imagine his mother burning these letters someplace where the desert flowers are "taller than men," and to render his father as "almost" redeemed by the apologies he tenders in this weekly ritual of regret and sorrow.

In addition to animating those with whom he grew up, Komunyakaa has continued to imaginatively construct the lives of other people. In "Buried Light," "Shrines," and other poems in the "Phantasmagoria" section of *Thieves of Paradise* (1998), undertaken after a 1990 return to Vietnam, Komunyakaa clothes himself in the various perspectives of Vietnamese peasants living in Vietnam, decades after the end of the United States' military engagement there. "Shrines" is particularly notable for the precision with which Komunyakaa suggests the destructiveness of Western influences upon Vietnamese culture.

In her seminal work *Fire in the Lake: The Vietnamese and the Americans in Vietnam* (1972), Frances Fitzgerald speculated that the greatest long-term resentment the people of Vietnam might have towards the United States and its policies would involve U.S. destruction of Vietnamese society. Forced resettlement, the destruction of productive land, and the rupture of community life had, even before the United States withdrew from Vietnam, combined to disorient the people of that nation. Fitzgerald writes that

> land had been the basis of social contract—the transmission belt of
> life that carried the generations of the family from the past into the
> future. Ancestor worshippers, the Vietnamese saw themselves as
> more than separate egos, as part of this continuum of life. As they
> took life from the earth and from the ancestors, so they would find

immortality in their children, who in their turn would take their place on the earth. To leave the land and the family forever was therefore to suffer a permanent, collective death.[17]

Yusef Komunyakaa's "Shrines," published 26 years after Fitzgerald's hypothesis, reflects the lingering dislocation and loss to which Fitzgerald alludes. Still living on the land, many Vietnamese have nonetheless *left* the land, feeling little connection to it or to their ancestors. And while Fitzgerald noted that during the war in Vietnam "the village *dinh* or shrine still stood in many of the villages of the south as testimony to the endurance of the traditional political design of the nation,"[18] Komunyakaa shows us the loss of that tradition:

> A few nightbirds scissors dusk into silhouettes ... distant voices harmonize silences. Thatched houses squat against darkness, and the squares of light grow through doorways like boxes inside boxes. They've driven ancestors deeper into the jungles, away from offerings of rice and children's laughter. There's no serpent to guard these new shrines. The cameraman has tried to make an amputee whole again, as if he can see through a lover's eyes. Everything's paralyzed at twilight, except the ghostly jitterbug-flicker of videos from Hong Kong, Thailand, and America, with spellbound faces in Hanoi, Haiphong, Quang Tri, wherever electricity goes. The abyss is under the index finger on the remote control. As if losing the gift of speech, they fall asleep inside someone else's dream.[19]

Komunyakaa deploys a painter's eye in seeing and animating this scene of loss and suspended animation. In less precise hands "Shrines" might be simply another poem deploring the misfit between the remains of Vietnam's traditional values, such as ancestor worship, and pervasive Western influence. In this case, the erosion of Vietnamese tradition results, at least in part, from advanced video technologies that both capture people's images and render other, fantasy images to them. There is "no serpent to guard these new shrines," but what, indeed, are these shrines, except televisions sets? The ghosts of past generations are lost and neglected, unable to nurture Vietnam's future, because those with electricity, like people everywhere else, have fallen in love with the fantasies that flicker on television screens. The Vietnamese people of this poem consume images and packaged stories, from "Hong Kong, Thailand, and America," foreign countries with foreign stories and foreign conventions, and they become more and more unmoored from the stories and ghosts that sustained even their own immediate ancestors.

The Vietnamese fought and won against China's, France's, and the United States' colonizing efforts in turn, seeking to preserve their autonomy, their language, their culture, and their world vision. In "Shrines," Komunyakaa offers the intriguing possibility that the Vietnamese struggle for autonomy has been defeated by television, which paralyzes everything in the evening, except for the "ghostly jitterbug-flicker" of videos. The same technology "tries to make an amputee whole again," to create a consumable image, a palatable story, about the Vietnam War. That story will be transmitted around the world and, perhaps, back to these people who sit "wherever electricity goes." Television watchers will see this amputee, who sits among them, with new eyes once he has been defined and interpreted by the television's narrative. It is a singular irony few poets could render so succinctly: a nation of people who fought so hard and so successfully to maintain independence and retain their language and ways of thought, now "fall[s] asleep inside someone else's dream," "as if losing the gift of speech." Vietnam may be an independent political entity, but its people have nonetheless been colonized by other countries. They have lost much of what they battled to protect, and a constant diet of television has seduced the population away from resistance to colonizing forces, effectively distracting, if not winning, their hearts and minds.

The first line of "Unnatural State of the Unicorn," the opening poem of *I Apologize For the Eyes in My Head* is the injunction to "Introduce me first as a man." Each volume that Komunyakaa has produced since 1986 has been a recapitulation of that demand. Without any attempt at Anatole Broyard's racial recusal, Yusef Komunyakaa has built a body of work in which his personal experience as an African American, Southern, working-class Vietnam War veteran has broadened, not limited, his imagination. No attentive reader could accuse Yusef Komunyakaa of being "merely a Negro; or even, merely a Negro writer." And yet Komunyakaa has never attempted to deny or efface his race. He has rendered the subjectivities of "others," whether female rape victims or regretful fathers, with insight, restraint, grace and humanity. The *specialness* of Komunyakaa's experiences as an African American man in the United States have whetted his appreciation for the concrete realities of people we seldom hear about in poetry (Vietnamese women; factory workers; abusive husbands; mutilated civilians). What we get from Komunyakaa is a determined balance and precision, as well as an even-handed view of lives in progress. The lives Komunyakaa examines are bounded by war, by violence, and by the atrocity we humans are so able to visit on each other; however, Komunyakaa's empathy invests his subjects with terrible beauty.

In the end, the choice devolves to readers as much as to writers. Do readers continue to make whiteness the "default position" for individuality, thus perceiving authors such as Yusef Komunyakaa as either raceless scribes or as lyrical sociologists? Or do we really pay attention, learning to empathize as readers in the same ways our finest writers have trained themselves to do? Readers' preoccupation with race, to the exclusion of all other things, caused Baldwin and Broyard untold anguish, and also robbed readers of the gifts these authors could have provided, had they not been so hamstrung by the world's race-based expectations. Still, denial of race, and of its centrality in American life, is a convenient and lazy fiction, and will, too, diminish readers and writers. Between these two unsatisfactory extremes stands Yusef Komunyakaa, who seeks to expand his and his readers' understanding of humanity, inhumanity, and the ways our individual *specialness* (to return to James Baldwin) can connect us to each other.

NOTES

1. Quoted in Edward Hirsch, *How to Read a Poem: and Fall in Love With Poetry* (New York: Harcourt, Brace, 1999), 225.
2. Henry Louis Gates, Jr., "The Passing of Anatole Broyard," in *13 Ways of Looking at a Black Man* (New York: Random House, 1997), 208.
3. Susan Gubar, *Racechanges: White Skin, Black Face in American Culture* (New York: Oxford University Press, 1997), 20.
4. Robert Hayden, ed., *Kaleidoscope: Poems by American Negro Poets* (New York: Harcourt, Brace, 1967), xix–xx.
5. In "'Lines of Tempered Steel': An Interview with Yusef Komunyakaa," by Vincente F. Gotera. Originally published in *Callaloo* 13.2 (1990): 215–29, the interview is reprinted in Komunyakaa's *Blue Notes: Essays, Interviews and Commentaries*, 59–75. The discussion of Baldwin is on pages 59–60.
6. Komunyakaa knew about African American authors from an early age. Even when a reader, rather than a writer, he was familiar with the Black Arts Movement, with LANGUAGE poetry, and with the many changes occurring in the literary world. His youthful knowledge of the works of African American authors, including Wheatley, Wright, Baldwin, and Brooks, stands in stark contrast to the experience outlined by author Walter Dean Myers in *Bad Boy: A Memoir* (New York: HarperCollins, 2001). Remembering himself as a young aspiring writer, Myers notes:

> My role models for writing were the ones we learned about in school. If an Englishman could appreciate beauty, why couldn't I? If Shakespeare could write about love and jealousy and hatreds, why couldn't I? At thirteen I had never read a book by a Negro writer. Perhaps they had some at the George Bruce Branch, but I didn't want to identify myself as a Negro by asking. (86)

Myers was born in 1937, a mere ten years before Komunyakaa, but grew up without the comforting knowledge of an African American literary tradition he might join. Indeed, it is the redoubtable Shakespeare against whom Myers measures himself, a writer deemed to be as "universal" as Myers would be "particular."
7. Author interview, Monday, June 28, 1999.
8. It is worth noting Bernard W. Quetchenbach's observation that "It may appear that the development of current identity poetics constitutes an intensification

of the individualism of contemporary poetry because the background of the poet is central to the engendering and experience of the poem. . . . But it is not so much the writer's identity that is important as it is the reader's identity, or the subject of identity itself." In Bryson, ed., *Ecopoems*, 248.

9. Komunyakaa, *I Apologize*, 3.

10. *Black Male: Representations of Masculinity in Contemporary American Art*, ed. Thelma Golden (New York: Harry N. Abrams, 1994), is an excellent source of analyses about this matter, as it manifests itself in the visual arts. Golden's own essay "My Brother" (19–43) is a lucid examination of the ways in which the black male body is appropriated, troped, and emptied of humanity by a society obsessed with policing or gazing upon such bodies. Golden's most trenchant observation is that "one of the greatest inventions of the twentieth century is the African American male—'invented' because black masculinity represents an amalgam of fears and projections in the American psyche which rarely conveys or contains the trope of truth about the black male's existence" (19). Komunyakaa uses words, arranged upon the page, alluding to history and art, and echoing in the reader's mind, to "convey . . . the trope of truth about the black male's existence." Or, more specifically, about his own black male existence.

11. Katarzyna Jakubiak offers an intriguing reading of "Unnatural State of the Unicorn" in her M.A. thesis, "Yusef Komunyakaa: Questioning Traditional Metaphors of Light and Darkness" (University of Northern Iowa, May 1999). Jakubiak notes that in this poem

> Komunyakaa makes use of the conventional metaphors HUMAN BODY IS THE CONTAINER FOR SOUL and SOUL IS AN ENTITY INSIDE THE BODY. However, saying "Inside my skin, / loving you, I am this space / my body believes in," Komunyakaa questions the conventional metaphors with the scientific knowledge that the only 'entity' inside from the body apart from anatomical organs is 'space.' Thus, questioning the metaphor of soul, Komunyakaa seems to call for another more adequate metaphor, which will show that there is something independent from 'skin' and invisible as 'space' which makes us all human. (16)

In short, Komunyakaa deftly uses and deflates conventional Western and African American conceptions about 'skin,' 'space,' and 'soul.' In so doing, he points to a common humanity, but not the fuzzy, elision-ridden commonality so many thinkers aspire to.

12. Komunyakaa, *Dien Cai Dau*, 17.

13. Komunyakaa, *Magic City*, 15.

14. Mercer and Julien, in Golden, ed., *Black Male*, 196.

15. Komunyakaa, *Magic City*, 43.

16. Louise Gluck, *Proofs and Theories: Essays on Poetry* (Hopewell, NJ: Ecco Press, 1994), 55.

17. Frances Fitzgerald, *Fire in the Lake: The Vietnamese and the Americans in Vietnam* (Boston: Little, Brown, 1972), 429–30.

18. Ibid.

19. Komunyakaa, *Thieves*, 82.

JAMES SMETHURST

The Black Arts Movement and Historically Black Colleges and Universities

Discussions of the Black Arts Movement of the 1960s and 1970s rarely give much consideration to black cultural activity in the South. This lack of interest is not only a feature of our own time. At the height of the movement, southern black artists and intellectuals complained about how difficult it was to attract the attention of their counterparts in the Northeast, the Midwest, and the West, even with the tremendous symbolic significance that the region retained in African American history and culture.[1] Yet despite this past and present scholarly inattention, Black Arts organizations, institutions, and events in the South were among the most successful grassroots black cultural efforts. These efforts made a powerful, and in many ways lasting, local impression in the South. At the same time, they were also central in promoting Black Arts as a truly national movement—national in the sense of bringing together activists from across the United States (and beyond) as well as in that of broadly embodying and articulating the concerns and the existence of a black nation.

Many of the political and cultural institutions of Reconstruction in the South had been destroyed by the disenfranchisement of most black southerners and the establishment of Jim Crow, but one legacy of Reconstruction and what might be thought of as the Reconstruction spirit still thrived in the 1950s and early 1960s: the historically black colleges and universities. The vast majority

From *New Thoughts on the Black Arts Movement,* edited by Lisa Gail Collins and Margo Natalie Crawford, pp. 75–91. Copyright © 2006 by Rutgers, The State University.

105

of these were located below the Mason-Dixon Line—though some important schools, notably Lincoln University, Cheney Training School for Teachers, and Central State University, were up North, and others, such as Howard University and Morgan State University, were to be found in such regionally ambiguous cities as Washington, D.C. and Baltimore. Since de jure segregation still operated in the South (and beyond) and de facto segregation or token integration was in effect at many colleges and universities elsewhere, a huge proportion of black college students (and black faculty) were concentrated at the African American schools in the South and the so-called Border States.

These concentrations of black schools and African American college students along with the national focus of the Civil Rights Movement on voting rights and the segregation of public facilities in the region left a deep imprint on the Black Arts Movement there. Of course, if we take Black Arts to be essentially the cultural wing of the Black Power Movement, the distinction between it and the Civil Rights Movement is difficult to draw precisely—perhaps more difficult than in any other region of the United States. To generalize broadly, the Civil Rights Movement of the late 1950s and early 1960s aimed in the first place at dismantling the segregation of public institutions and public accommodations and at the enfranchisement of African Americans across the South. Black Power was a contentious political formation, but generally speaking nearly all its manifestations involved a concept of liberation and self-determination, whether in a separate republic (e.g., the "Black Belt" of the South), some sort of federated state, black-run city (Detroit, for example), or some smaller community unit (say, Harlem, East Los Angeles, or the Central Ward of Newark). Black Power also generally entailed some notion of the development or recovery of a politically engaged "national" culture, often linked to an already existing folk or popular culture—in short, Black Arts. Yet this account oversimplifies things since it suggests that Black Arts simply issued from Black Power when both movements arose more or less simultaneously. Early Black Arts and proto-Black Arts institutions, such as the Umbra Poets Workshop, Black Arts/West, the Black Arts Repertory Theater/School (BARTS), the Free Southern Theater, and the Organization of Black American Culture (OBAC), played crucial roles in the development of important Black Power organizations and institutions in their regions. In fact, many of the best known Black Arts activists, such as Amiri Baraka, Haki Madhubuti, Askia Touré, and Larry Neal, were among the most important Black Power leaders. Similarly, if, as Amiri Baraka notes, the movement included many artists with an interest in politics, such as poet Sonia Sanchez, Neal, Touré, and Baraka himself, it also contained many political leaders with backgrounds in the arts, such as the Revolutionary Action

Movement leader Muhammad Ahmad and Black Panther Party for Self-Defense founder Bobby Seale.[2]

Given the concentration of African Americans in the Deep South, Civil Rights efforts, particularly around voting rights, were always concerned with the issues of black political self-determination, black power if you will, that would come to be the hallmark of Black Power in its various manifestations. Thus, it is not surprising that Civil Rights organizations, most famously the Student Non-Violent Coordinating Committee (SNCC), played a central role in the development of the notion of Black Power and the Black Power Movement in the mid-1960s. Similarly, the considerable lag between legislation, federal policy decisions, and Supreme Court cases in Washington and the actual dismantling of old-style Jim Crow in the South during the late 1960s and early 1970s caused militant Black Power organizations on southern black campuses and in southern African American communities to concern themselves with issues of essentially de jure segregation that are more usually associated with the earlier Civil Rights Movement. Also, as writer Kalamu ya Salaam points out, the focus on electing black officials that emerged from the landmark 1972 National Black Political Convention in Gary, Indiana, necessitated a new Black Power orientation toward the South since the demographics of the region presented the greatest black electoral possibilities.[3] Again, this often meant that the resulting campaigns took on the tenor, the tactics, and often the goals of the Civil Rights Movement in order to have a chance of success. In fact, they *were* both civil rights and Black Power efforts, aiming at the final end of legal or quasi-legal Jim Crow and black self-determination at the same time—though, of course, one might argue that this had always been the case, especially in areas, such as many of the counties of the Mississippi Delta, where African Americans formed the overwhelming majority of the population.

Even the line between Civil Rights and Black Arts cultural institutions in the South is often quite fuzzy. Such institutions as the SNCC Freedom Singers and the Free Southern Theater were not, as northern black cultural institutions generally were, simply supportive of the southern Civil Rights Movement, they were actually prominent features of the movement. Though racked by personal and political contradictions throughout its existence, the Free Southern Theater (FST), founded in 1963 on the campus of historically black Tougaloo College in Mississippi, was the most important progenitor of community-based Black Arts activity in the South. As will be noted later, ironically, given the place of the theater's origin, the community-oriented southern cities in which the FST sparked the most successful regional manifestation of Black Arts, such as New Orleans (where the FST moved in

1965), Houston, Miami, and Memphis, remained relatively detached from the more prominent black campuses.

There was a symbiotic relationship between the educational institutions and Civil Rights—a relationship that significantly molded the movement and changed the institutions. Though the administrations, and often the faculties, were initially cautious or indifferent in their public relationship to the movement, the students of these institutions formed much of the core leadership and rank and file of the movement in the South. Students from southern black schools were instrumental in local sit-ins, picket lines, boycotts, and demonstrations, particularly in the 1960 sit-in movement that swept the South (and much of the North), coalescing into SNCC. Sometimes these young people organized under the auspices of established groups, such as the NAACP Youth Council or the Southern Christian Leadership Council (SCLC), and sometimes they created their own local organizations. As leading Black Arts activists Amiri Baraka, Kalamu ya Salaam, and Askia Touré have noted, these students inspired young black activists, artists, and intellectuals elsewhere in the United States (often themselves, like Baraka, poet and critic A. B. Spellman, poet, playwright, critic, and scholar Larry Neal, and Muhammad Ahmad, alumni of historically black schools) through their boldness, their militancy, and their refusal to wait for established leaders.[4]

A tremendous number of Black Arts activists, including many from outside the South, were politicized and introduced to a distinctly African American cultural tradition while at historically African American colleges and universities as students or faculty members (or both). Similarly, numerous younger black artists and intellectuals in San Francisco, Oakland, Los Angeles, Chicago, Detroit, Cleveland, New York, New Orleans, Washington, D.C. and so on, such as the writers Jayne Cortez, Tom Dent, David Llorens, Dingane Joe Goncalves (editor of the vital Black Arts magazine, *Journal of Black Poetry*), Sonia Sanchez, Kalamu ya Salaam, Ed Spriggs, Michael Thelwell, Askia Touré, Ebon Dooley, Haki Madhubuti, and Sterling Plumpp were active participants in SNCC, CORE, and other militant direct action civil rights groups that drew heavily on students from historically black campuses. Even those of this cohort of activist artists and intellectuals who never worked in the South or attended historically black schools, belonging instead to northern affiliates of the major Civil Rights groups or local organizations, generally saw themselves as both supporting the southern student movement and bringing that movement North to confront racism in their own regions. At the same time that they were energized by the southern movement, many future Black Arts activists who did go South (or were already in the South), tried to further radicalize the southern movement, introducing or reinforcing radical and/or nationalist thinking within SNCC and other civil rights organizations. Thus, while the Black Arts institutions and activities of the South had difficulty attracting attention beyond the region, the South was, nonetheless, far more crucial symbolically and practically to the development of the national movement than has sometimes been acknowledged.[5] At the same time, within the South itself, there was a distinction in style and orientation among cities such as Houston, New Orleans, and Miami where the Black Arts Movement was rooted largely in communities and other cities, such as Atlanta, Washington, D.C., Baton Rouge, and Nashville, where the movement was based more on the campus.[6]

The administrations of the historically African American schools in the South and in Washington, D.C., especially those dependent on public funding, were politically cautious and even conservative during the period immediately before and during the Cold War. A notorious example of such caution, if not cowardice, in the face of the emerging red scare was the firing of W.E.B. Du Bois from the faculty of Atlanta University in 1944. On a less public level, another sign of institutional conservatism was the exodus of many progressive and Left faculty members from historically black schools in the South during the late 1940s and the 1950s.[7] While administrators often sympathized with the sentiments and goals of the student movement that erupted in their institutions in 1960, under explicit or implicit pressure from the local and state power structure they frequently tried to rein in student protest, in some cases threatening to discipline or actually disciplining demonstrators—as when the Southern University expelled seven students (including the senior class president Marvin Robinson) arrested at a 1960 sit-in in Baton Rouge. And, however sympathetic these administrators might be, they often had a far different vision of appropriate tactics and even what goals were feasible than had the young demonstrators.[8] Even Martin Luther King, Jr. was unable to realize his long-held desire of being appointed to the Board of Trustees of his alma mater, Morehouse College, due largely to his perceived radicalism—particularly after King came out publicly against the United States' involvement in the Vietnam War.[9] As novelist John O. Killens noted while describing his experience as a writer-in-residence at Fisk, not only did early Black Power and Black Arts supporters have to contend with conservative (and often white) trustees and nervous (often black) administrators, but also conservative and liberal faculty members who saw "Fisk as a finishing school to train black boys and girls how to be nice little young white ladies and gentlemen in black skins" (63). These faculty members were notably hostile to Black Power and Black Arts, though often they attacked those movements passively or covertly. Killens recalls that when he organized the Black Writers' Conferences at Fisk, which were, as will be discussed below, landmarks in defining the existence and the shape of the emerging Black Arts movement and featured many leading older and younger black writers and scholars, the heads of the Fisk English, Speech, and Drama Departments did not attend.[10]

The administrations of many historically black schools took an extremely paternalistic and condescending stance toward their students, even at such elite schools as Howard.[11] Ironically, as was the case on many predominantly white campuses, such as the University of California at Berkeley, this sort of heavy-handed paternalism actually strengthened, and, in the case of Central State University in Ohio, inspired student activism by stoking general student dissatisfaction and creating broad support for relatively radical organizations, such as the earliest formation of the Revolutionary Action Movement at Central State in 1962.[12]

Nonetheless, such schools were often willing to hire (or retain) intellectuals, such as John O. Killens (Fisk University), poet and novelist Margaret Walker (Jackson State University), poet Melvin Tolson (Wiley College and Langston University), poet and scholar Sterling Brown (Howard University), critic and scholar Mercer Cook (Howard), poet, playwright, and director Owen Dodson (Howard), and poet Lance Jeffers (Howard), who had been part of the Popular Front subculture of the 1930s and 1940s, supporting organizations and events initiated by the Communist Party—and sometimes, like Walker, actually belonging to the Party. In some cases (as in Killens'), these faculty members still retained live connections to what remained of the cultural and political institutions of the Communist Left. Others were more distant from public support of Left initiatives and organizations in the 1950s and the early 1960s, but remained essentially unrepentant as to their political activities during the 1930s and 1940s—as did Walker, Brown, and Tolson. And quite a few of these veterans of 1930s and 1940s radicalism supported the journal *Freedomways*, conceived and founded by such prominent African American leftists as Louis Burnham, W.E.B. Du Bois, Shirley Graham Du Bois, Esther Cooper Jackson, and Margaret Burroughs, when it appeared in 1961, joining the editorial board and/or contributing stories, essays, poems, art work, and so on.

Not only did black colleges sometimes hire faculty with radical pasts (and presents), they also supported large-scale literary events initiated by intellectuals with some past or present connection to the Left. For example, Rosey Pool was a leftwing Dutch journalist and scholar living in Britain during the late 1950s and early 1960s. Her 1962 anthology, *Beyond the Blues*, the first serious anthology of contemporary African American poetry in more than a decade, highlighted politically and formally radical black writing.[13] Pool organized a festival of African American poetry at Alabama A & M in 1964 and again in 1966—though the featured participants were drawn from

Pool's connections in the Midwest (e.g., Margaret Burroughs, Dudley Randall, Margaret Danner, and Mari Evans) where she spent much time while assembling her anthology rather than in the South. Pool also lectured on African American poetry at dozens of historically black campuses in 1959–1960. These festivals as well as Pool's lectures did much to create a sense of the emergence of a new black poetry that was both formally and politically radical. And, again, it needs to be noted that because the historically black schools drew on a national (and international) network of students and alumni, these sorts of events had an impact far beyond the South.

It is true that some schools, as was the case with Howard apparently, protected their faculty from various Red hunters with the understanding that they would not engage in high profile radical politics. Still, despite this limited and limiting resistance to McCarthyism, there were not many historically white universities where a professor who had been engaged in the activities of the Popular Front as publicly as had Sterling Brown could have survived without repenting of his or her political past (and sometimes even a public repentance would not save the former leftist). While many of the scholars and artists teaching in historically black schools had willingly, or under institutional duress, retreated from political activism, many became energized by the revived Civil Rights Movement, especially the Black Student Movement that in 1960 exploded after four North Carolina A & T freshmen sat-in at a downtown Greensboro, North Carolina Woolworth's lunch counter. This older generation of radicals helped open political and cultural spaces that were crucial to the development of what might be thought of as a Black Arts/Black Power cadre, especially in conjunction with the domestic and international currents of civil rights, nationalism, and national liberation that flowed together on historically black campuses in a distinctive way.

Interestingly, with the exception of peripheral Black Arts participant Julian Bond, few of those who would spearhead the Black Arts Movement participated directly in the early Black Student Movement in the South—though many would join CORE, SNCC, and other civil rights organizations in the North and the West. However, as noted earlier, a number such as Tom Dent, poet Calvin Hernton, Amiri Baraka, Larry Neal, A. B. Spellman, and poet and critic Sarah Webster Fabio attended historically black universities in the decade before 1960. Many of these writers found what they considered to be the generally cautious and accommodationist atmosphere of most historically black schools alienating. However, they also often discovered a sense of African American folk and popular culture and history as subjects that could be approached in an engaged and intellectually serious manner—though often this education took place outside the formal circuits of the institution. For example, Amiri Baraka recalls Howard as being "an employment agency at best, at worst a kind of church ... for a small accommodationist black middle class."[14] Yet he also cites Sterling Brown's classes on African American music, also attended by A. B. Spellman, as "opening us to the fact that the music could be studied and, by implication, that black people had a history. He was raising the music as an art, a thing for scholarship and research as well as deep enjoyment."[15] Baraka and Spellman, in turn, would become leading Black Arts proponents of the notion of a black cultural continuum that included folk, popular, and avant-garde elements. Similarly, Tom Dent remembered that watching historian Benjamin Quarles working in the library of Dillard University gave him a sense that a serious intellectual life was possible.[16]

There was also a long tradition of civil rights activism at some historically black schools, particularly Howard and Fisk. Howard students, for example, had been instrumental in launching the campaign against Jim Crow in public facilities and accommodations during the 1940s, using many of the tactics of later activists, including sitting-in at lunch counters, and suffering much the same resistance from the Howard administration.[17] Given the inevitable turnover of students and the disinterest of college administrations in publicly acknowledging such past militancy, radical faculty often served as unofficial historians. In addition to introducing African American culture as a subject of serious study, Sterling Brown revealed to members of the Non-Violent Action Group (NAG), the SNCC affiliate on campus during the early 1960s, Howard's considerable history as a center of black political activism and radical thought as well as the sort of roadblocks previous administrations had presented to that radicalism—much like the resistance that NAG encountered in their own time.[18]

Also, the historically black schools drew a large international student body, especially from Africa and the Caribbean. A number of these students were radicals, sometimes Marxists or influenced by Marxism, and engaged with the liberation movements in their home countries and throughout Asia, Africa, the Caribbean, and Latin America. These international students were limited in their ability to participate directly in U.S. political movements by their legal status. However, through them native-born African Americans more closely encountered Post-Bandung Conference liberation movements and various strains of radicalism, Pan-Africanism, different sorts of communism and socialism, and militant anti-imperialism, than was the case on most U.S. campuses in the late 1950s and early 1960s.[19]

In turn, the students from the United States who became active in campus politics often had some experience in black nationalist organizations, particularly the Nation of Islam, and/or the Civil Rights Movement. Some at Central State, Howard, and other schools outside of the Deep South, such as Ed Brown at Howard, had been expelled from southern historically black schools for their civil rights activism. Others brought some background in various sorts of Left organizations with them. For example, Kwame Ture (Stokely Carmichael) came to Howard from New York City in 1960 with much exposure to Marxism. In part through his close friendship with fellow Bronx Science High School student Gene Dennis (son of the Communist Party national chairman Eugene Dennis), and through his membership in a progressive Bronx science student group, Ture met a number of leading black Communists, including Benjamin Davis (the well-known former City Councilperson from Harlem), and had participated in a range of Communist and Socialist activities and institutions.[20] Tom Kahn, a gay white Howard student and a leader of the Young People's Socialist League affiliated with the Socialist Party, worked closely with Ture in NAG. Kahn eventually became the head of the League for Industrial Democracy, the original parent organization of Students for a Democratic Society (SDS). Kahn brought not only his radical politics with him, but also a close friendship with the older gay African American Socialist Bayard Rustin who became a key adviser of NAG and, later, SNCC—though Kahn, like Rustin, later moved to the right end of the socialist political spectrum.

This encounter between the international independence movements and various strains of U.S. radicalism and activism was particularly intense at Howard University where the mix of black students from all the regions of the United States, Africa, and the English-speaking Caribbean was more diverse than at any other American college or university. As newly self-governing African, Asian, and Caribbean nations opened embassies in Washington, D.C., especially after the independence of Ghana in 1957, Howard students, many of whom were citizens of the newly independent nations, were invited to parties, lectures, receptions, and so on, at these embassies. This direct connection of Howard students to independence leaders of the often revolutionary new governments energized politically minded Howard students and, again, expanded their political horizons in a manner that was unique. In addition to the direct impact on political thought on campus, the international students and, at Howard, the direct links to the new states of the former colonial world also provided students at historically black schools a sophistication with respect to the possibilities of black culture and models of politically engaged art that were hard to come by on what might be thought of as historically white campuses in the later 1950s and early 1960s.[21] Not surprisingly, Howard became a particular locus of Left nationalist influence within SNCC and the Black Student Movement.

As mentioned earlier, a number of important black writers worked as teachers at the black colleges and universities in the South during the late

1950s and early 1960s. A very high percentage had radical pasts. Some like Robert Hayden had moved considerably from their earlier Left politics—though Hayden's continuing engagement with history in his work showed a link to his earlier Left poetry of *Heart-Shape in the Dust* (1940). Others, as previously noted, such as Margaret Walker, Sterling Brown, and John O. Killens, stayed much closer to their earlier Left commitments. Killens' writers' workshop at Fisk University was a particularly significant catalyst of the early Black Arts Movement during the middle 1960s. A number of important Black Arts writers, most notably Nikki Giovanni, were members of the workshop. Like other older radical writers, including Margaret Walker at Jackson State University and Sterling Brown at Howard University, Killens saw one of his main tasks in mentoring young black writers and political activists as reminding them of their artistic and political ancestors, especially those associated with the Popular Front era.[22] When Killens returned to New York in the late 1960s, the workshop continued under Donald Lee Graham (Le Graham) until Graham's death in 1971.

Fisk, of course, was the home of other important black poets, most notably Hayden and Arna Bontemps. Nonetheless, it was Killens and his workshop that figured most prominently in initiating the writers' conferences at Fisk in 1966 and 1967. These conferences were watershed events marking the emergence of the Black Arts Movement as the ascendant force in African American letters. Such older artists and scholars as Ossie Davis, Saunders Redding, Bontemps, Hayden, Margaret Walker, Loften Mitchell, and Melvin Tolson dominated the first conference. Virtually the only younger writer to appear on the program of the conference was the novelist Melvin Kelley—apparently Baraka was invited, but did not attend. However, the new militant nationalist writing made itself felt everywhere at the conference as participants obsessively mentioned Baraka and other younger writers, either disapprovingly or as the wave of the future (or often both). Some older writers took up the banner of the new militants, as did Walker in her reading of a poem to Malcolm X, and as did Tolson during his famous debate with Robert Hayden in which he asserted, "I'm a black poet, an African-American poet, a Negro poet," in response to Hayden's claim that "he was a poet who happens to be Negro." It was also at this conference that a chance meeting between Walker, Dudley Randall, and Margaret Burroughs resulted in Broadside Press's first book project, the seminal anthology *For Malcolm* (1969).[23]

Younger writers, particularly Baraka and Detroit playwright Ron Milner, one of the most important Black Arts theater workers, dominated the 1967 Fisk conference. Older writers, including Killens, Brooks, Danner, and scholar John Henrik Clarke, actively took part in the conference. However, these literary elders were among the most enthusiastic supporters of the new black writing. A number of those older artists not previously identified with the new cultural and political militancy, most famously Gwendolyn Brooks, publicly embraced Black Power and Black Arts at the conference. In fact, these conversions, particularly that of Brooks, gave the conference much of its charge as an event marking a new day in African American letters. Those artists who had seemed to oppose or express doubts about the emerging national political/artistic movements at the earlier conference were for the most part absent or far less prominent. For example, Hayden did not participate directly in the conference—though he was a featured artist during the week of cultural events at Fisk. Despite the fact that the older writers were among the most sympathetic to the new militant literary nationalism, the younger members of the audience frequently took them to task. Though these attacks might have been unfair, reflecting in the view of a *Negro Digest* correspondent the ignorance of the attackers as to the work of those they attacked, nonetheless they demonstrated a much changed atmosphere from the previous year when the Black Arts Movement was more like a haunting presence.[24]

At Howard, Sterling Brown played much the same mentoring role as did Killens at Fisk—though with his own distinct style. One of his students from the early 1960s, the fiction writer and NAG member Mike Thelwell (author of the novel *The Harder They Come* [1980]), recalled that Brown's formal classes were extremely competent, but more or less standard literature courses of the day—though not entirely so since it was not unheard of for someone like pianist Willie "The Lion" Smith to show up at Brown's classes. However, as noted earlier, Brown's unofficial seminars and discussion sessions (with bourbon) on African American culture, history, music, literature, and politics, nurtured and inspired many Black Arts and Black Power activists (and also pre- and post-Black Arts writers) including Amiri Baraka, A. B. Spellman, Toni Morrison, and Thelwell. Brown also served as a mentor to the largely avant-gardist literary grouping around the student journal *Dasein*, including Percy Johnston, Oswald Govan, Walter De Legall, and Leroy Stone, as well as to the political activists in NAG, including Thelwell, Kwame Ture, Cleveland Sellers, Ed Brown, Rap Brown, Charlie Cobb, and Courtland Cox, who would play a key role in the leadership of SNCC and the emergence of Black Power.[25] While the *Dasein* group did not participate directly in the political activities of NAG and SNCC (and while the NAG activists considered the Howard Poets to be bohemians a little too concerned with their images as artists), the active existence of both groups contributed to a sense of a dynamic political and cultural environment on campus. At the same time, the fact that neither NAG nor *Dasein* were ever officially recognized by Howard highlights some of the contradictions of political and cultural life on historically black campuses in the early 1960s.[26]

The relatively modest campus venues for formally and politically radical black art and Left and/or nationalist politics took on a new significance as a mass constituency for the Black Power Movement and the Black Arts Movement grew in the general population of African Americans in the South as well as among black intellectuals and students. As young African Americans (as well as older African Americans) in the South became frustrated with the unwillingness or the open resistance of the white southern power structure to go beyond the desegregation of public facilities and to allow the black community full access to economic, educational, and political opportunities, militant Black Power groups emerged in neighborhoods and especially on the college campuses of such black schools as Southern University, North Carolina A & T, South Carolina State, and Jackson State. This led to the creation of important Black Power/Black Arts institutions, such as Malcolm X University (established in Durham, North Carolina, in 1969 and moving to Greensboro in 1970) and Student Organization for Black Unity (SOBU) (the most important national Black Power student organization, founded in Greensboro in 1969). The activities of these militant campus groups, especially at more working-class campuses, such as North Carolina A & T and South Carolina State, often revolved around neighborhood concerns, such as housing and school systems, as well as general concerns about the persistence of blatant Jim Crow practices, especially by white merchants. There was an extremely negative and often violent response to these activities by local authorities, leading to the death of students at Southern University, South Carolina State, and Jackson State at the hands of National Guardsmen or law enforcement agents. The extreme responses of the police and the local and state political establishments further radicalized students and faculty at the historically black schools.[27]

As a result of this new constituency for radical nationalist ideas, institutions, and activities on campus and in the broader black community, the historically black schools were increasingly willing to provide institutional support for Black Arts or Black Arts-influenced activities and institutions. In part, this was because the increased political engagement (or the willingness to make open their political engagement) of the faculty propelled this institutional support. After the Fisk conferences and the Alabama A & T conferences, the historically black colleges frequently hosted conferences and festivals of African American art and literature, including the annual Black Poetry Festivals at Southern University beginning in 1972 and the Phillis Wheatley Bicentennial Festival at Jackson State in 1973.[28]

In addition to this willingness to host Black Arts or Black Arts-influenced events, many historically African American schools hired Black Arts writers, artists, and scholars as permanent or visiting faculty. A very incomplete list

would include poets Haki Madhubuti and Amos Zu-Bolton, OBAC paint-
ers Jeff Donaldson and Wadsworth Jarrell, and critic Stephen Henderson
at Howard, poets Calvin Hernton and Jay Wright at Talladega, poet (and
African National Congress activist in exile) Keorapetse Kgositsile, poets Jay
Wright and Andre Lorde at Tougaloo, poet and critic A. B. Spellman and
Henderson (before his departure to Howard) at Morehouse, poet and literary historian Eugene Redmond at Southern, and poet Donald Lee Graham
at Fisk (taking over John Killens' Black Writers Workshop). In a number of
cases, such as those of Henderson and Donaldson at Howard, these faculty
members were hired essentially to remake departments in a Black Arts or
Black Power mode.

Atlanta with its neighboring Spelman, Morehouse, Clark, Atlanta University and Morris Brown College became an especially important locus of
Black Arts and Black Power artists and intellectuals. The concentration of
schools and, increasingly, artists and intellectuals, who participated in the
Black Arts Movement and the Black Power Movement and were often on
the faculty of one of the schools, led to the establishment of such institutions
as the Center for Black Art and the Institute of the Black World. These institutions were not connected to particular schools, but were made possible by
the sheer density of historically black colleges and universities and the new
level of acceptance of Black Arts and Black Power by the faculty and administrations of the schools.

The Institute of the Black World was at first affiliated with the Martin
Luther King, Jr. Memorial Center rather than one of the black colleges or
universities. Though the Institute eventually developed a focus on education
and the social sciences, it was imagined initially as a research-oriented hub of
the emerging Black Studies movement in academia with a strong interest in
furthering the Black Arts Movement. The Institute was largely the brainchild
of historian Vincent Harding, chair of the History Department at Spelman,
and Stephen Henderson, chair of the English Department at Morehouse.
Henderson's *Understanding the New Black Poetry* (1972), an "Institute of the
Black World Book," was the most prominent academic Black Arts statement
on African American poetics as well as an extremely influential anthology.

In fact, when listing the central concerns of the field of Black Studies in
the Institute's Statement of Purpose and Program, the second item of a list of
ten points concerned nationalist art:

> The encouragement of those creative artists who are searching for
> the meaning of a black aesthetic, who are now trying to define and
> build the basic ground on which black creativity may flow in the
> arts. Encounter among these artists on the one hand, and scholars,

activists, and students on the other, must be constant in both formal and informal settings.[29]

Again, though the Institute of the Black World was associated with the King Center, it would not have been possible without the black schools of University Center—a fact that is acknowledged in the statement.[30]

Even more grassroots-oriented initiatives, such as the Center for Black Art and the journal *Rhythm*, both largely organized by poet and critic A. B. Spellman (whose 1966 *Four Lives in the Bebop Business* remains a classic of jazz criticism) after his move to Atlanta, were largely based among the radicalized black university community and were aimed at an audience significantly outside the South. In fact, one finds a certain alienation or distance from the local communities, at least initially, by those, such as Spellman, who migrated South to work in the black schools of Atlanta. In a report on the Atlanta scene in *The Cricket*, a black arts music journal based in Newark and edited by Spellman, Amiri Baraka, and Larry Neal, Spellman clearly considers the music and arts scene in Atlanta to be backward—though he also found a rootedness in the black community of Atlanta that he felt New York lacked.[31]

Perhaps the greatest example of the strengths and weaknesses of the Black Arts Movement in Atlanta can be seen in the attempt of former *Black World* editor Hoyt Fuller and others to create a Black Power/Black Arts journal to replace *Black World*. With a readership in the tens of thousands, *Black World* had been the most important intellectual journal of the Black Arts and Black Power movements. Its parent company, Johnson Publications shut down *Black World* in 1976 after a heated debate over the alleged anti-semitism of the journal. Anti-semitism was only the ostensible issue in the debate. What was really in question was whether Johnson Publishing, which issued such popular magazines as *Ebony* and *Jet*, wanted to continue publishing a radical, though widely circulating, intellectual journal that did not make money. Of course, this had been an issue between Fuller and Johnson Publishing for years. However, the decline in the Black Power Movement, in part precipitated and certainly hastened by the internal battle in such key organizations as the Congress of African People (CAP), diminished and divided the audience of *Black World* (which was generally inclined toward the cultural nationalist side of the movement's internal struggles). As a result the considerable attempts to save the journal were not sufficiently unified and broad to successfully pressure Johnson Publishing into maintaining it.

The idea then was to create a new journal, *First World*, completely controlled by the movement that could carry on the work of *Black World* without depending on the financial support of an essentially unsympathetic owner.

Atlanta, Fuller's birthplace, seemed like an ideal location given its concentration of African American colleges and universities and radicalized black faculty, including Stephen Henderson and Fuller's close friend (and, later, literary executor) Richard Long, and its prominence as a national center of the Civil Rights Movement and Black Studies as embodied in the King Center and the Institute of the Black World. However, after a promising start in 1977, *First World* failed, publishing its last issue in 1980. Fuller's premature death in 1981 foreclosed hope that it might be revived.

In part, *First World* suffered from the divisions that caused the movement as a whole to decline nationally. After all, *First World* was hardly the only important black intellectual or cultural journal to disappear in that era. Much of the early impetus to initiate a journal to replace *Black World* took place outside Atlanta.[32] Still, part of *First World*'s failure was due not only to the decline of Black Power and Black Arts nationally, but due also to an inability to build a local support network in Atlanta much beyond University Center that replicated the sort of network in Chicago that was crucial to the success of *Black World*. This is a failure that characterized the cultural movement as a whole in Atlanta. For example, despite Atlanta's reputation as a premier center of black artistic activity in the South, no viable African American theater group developed outside the confines of University Center during the Black Arts era.[33]

As a result, Atlanta became an increasingly important national center of nationalist thought and activity without a concomitant growth of local grassroots institutions that reached much beyond University Center. It hosted the first Congress of African People (CAP) convention in 1970, a landmark in what historian Komozi Woodard has termed the "Modern Black Convention Movement." It was at the Atlanta Congress that the CAP was established as an ongoing umbrella group of a wide ideological range of black political and cultural groups—though radical nationalism dominated CAP until its effective demise as a result of factional battles between Marxists and cultural nationalists in the mid-1970s.[34] However, the Black Arts Movement in Atlanta seems to have been relatively unconnected to the less academically centered movements in the South. For example, Henderson's *Understanding the New Black Poetry* did not contain any work by the writers associated with BLKARTSOUTH in New Orleans, Sudan-Southwest in Houston, or the Afro Arts Theater in Miami. The poets living in the South that Henderson did include, such as A. B. Spellman, Donald L. Graham, Keorapetse Kgositsile, and Laedele X, were almost all based in the relatively elite historically black colleges and universities of Nashville, Atlanta, and Washington, D.C.—and the more academically oriented institutions connected to those schools. Similarly, Black Arts theater and cultural groups from Atlanta seem to have been relatively uninvolved in the Southern Black Cultural Alliance, a dynamic regional Black Arts umbrella organization that included Black Arts groups and theaters from Texas to Florida.

However, to dwell solely on the shortcomings and failures of the academically (and nationally) oriented focus of the Black Power and Black Arts Movements in Atlanta, Nashville, and other southern black academic centers is to miss the important role that these centers played. Conferences at such schools as Jackson State, Fisk, Alabama A & T, Tougaloo, and Southern early on gave visibility to new black writing and aired the national debates that had been largely restricted to study groups, workshops, and little magazines. In the late 1960s and the 1970s similar conferences at Howard and the University Center schools of Atlanta, notably the 1968 Toward a Black University conference, brought together leading radical black cultural and political leaders (who were often one and the same), again providing a sense of national (and even international) coherence to now intersecting spheres of black politics, education, and art.

Atlanta today is a national African American cultural and intellectual center that shows a major nationalist and activist influence in ways that would have seemed incredible before 1960. And if, as political scientist Adolph Reed suggests, radical black organizations were unable to offer alternatives to the "black regime" of Maynard Jackson in the 1970s and the 1980s that attracted broad support within the black community, artists who had been leading Black Arts activists spearheaded cultural initiatives that *did* reach a mass audience. The advocacy of poet Ebon Dooley, a veteran of Chicago's Organization of Black American Culture (OBAC), played a major role in extending Jackson's desire to be known as the "culture mayor" to cover grassroots arts activities in black neighborhoods.[35] One of these activities was the establishment of a black art museum, Hammonds House, in the 1980s by poet and visual artist Ed Spriggs, who had been a leader in a wide range of Black Arts institutions in New York (including the founding of The Studio Museum in Harlem), in a then declining West End neighborhood rather than downtown. It also led to Atlanta's regionally and nationally known Black Arts Festival.

It is in no small part due to the Black Arts Movement and its impact on the students, faculties, and even administrations of the historically black schools there that Atlanta has gained a prominence in national African American intellectual and cultural discussions that is often quite at odds with the tradition of pragmatism and conciliation often associated with its African American politicians. Similarly, while the cities of Nashville and Washington, D.C. lacked the same density of black educational institutions, the traditional prestige, large number of African and Caribbean students, and longstanding, if uneven, traditions of political activism of Fisk and Howard allowed them to make major contributions to the growth of Black Arts as a national movement with international ties. As a result of the concentration of black students, intellectuals, and artists politicized by the Civil Rights Movement, Black Power, and Black Arts in Atlanta, Nashville, Washington, and other southern African American educational centers, radical African American political and cultural activities in these cities inspired black artists inside and outside the region, promoting a sense of Black Arts as a coherent national movement.

NOTES

1. Kalamu ya Salaam, "Enriching the Paper Trail: An Interview with Tom Dent" *African American Review* 27: 2 (Summer 1993): 339; Kalamu ya Salaam, autobiographical statement (unpublished); author's interview with Kalamu ya Salaam, April 23, 2000, New Orleans, Louisiana.

2. Author's interview with Amiri Baraka, July 15, 2000, Newark, New Jersey.

3. Author's interview with Kalamu ya Salaam.

4. Amiri Baraka, *The Black Arts Movement* (Newark: self-published mimeograph, 1994), 1; author's interview with Amiri Baraka; author's interview with Askia Touré, December 2, 2000, Cambridge, Massachusetts; Kalamu ya Salaam, *The Magic of Juju: An Appreciation of the Black Arts Movement* (Chicago: Third World Press, forthcoming), 5.

5. For a discussion of the difficulty in reaching an audience beyond the region due to the parochialism of northern Black Arts activists and institutions, see Salaam, "Enriching the Paper Trail," 338–39.

6. This is not to say that educational institutions such as Dillard University (where Tom Dent's father, Albert Dent, was president) and Southern University–New Orleans, did not figure prominently in the Black Power and Black Arts movements of Houston, Miami, and New Orleans. Nonetheless, the community oriented BLKARTSOUTH in New Orleans and the groups it inspired, such as Sudan Arts Southwest in Houston and the Theatre of Afro Arts in Miami, were far more important in those cities than any institutions linked to a campus or group of campuses. These community-based groups formed the backbone of the Southern Black Cultural Alliance, the most successful regional Black Arts organization.

7. For example, Tom Dent notes the departure of progressive faculty members, such as L. D. Reddick and St. Clair Drake, and Left teachers, such as the visual artist Elizabeth Catlett, from Dillard University during the period. Tom Dent, "Marcus B. Christian: An Appreciation," *Black American Literature Forum* 18: 1 (Spring 1984): 25. Interestingly, historically black schools in the North, such as Central State University, Howard University, and Lincoln University, were often havens for progressive or Left faculty.

8. August Meier and Elliott Rudwick, *CORE: A Study in the Civil Rights Movement, 1942–1968* (New York: Oxford University Press, 1973), 107–108; David Harmon, *Beneath the Image of the Civil Rights Movement and Race Relations: Atlanta, Georgia, 1946–1981* (New York: Garland, 1996), 127–46; Jack Walker, "Sit-Ins in Atlanta: A Study in the Negro Revolt," in *Atlanta, Georgia, 1960–1961: Sit-Ins*

and Student Activism, ed. David J. Garrow (Brooklyn: Carlson Publishing, 1989), 64–76.

9. Michael Eric Dyson, *I May Not Get There With You: The True Martin Luther King, Jr.* (New York: Free Press, 2000), 255–56.

10. John O. Killens, "The Artist and the Black University," *The Black Scholar* 1: 1 (November 1969): 63.

11. Author's interview with Michael Thelwell, February 20, 2003, Pelham, Massachusetts; author's telephone interview with Muhammad Ahmad, August 20, 2002.

12. Author's interview with Muhammad Ahmad.

13. Pool, a frequent writer for the journal, *Soviet Woman*, was clearly active in the international Communist movement—though on what level it is hard to say precisely. Pool's correspondence with such poets as Sam Allen, Chuck Anderson, Mari Evans, and Sarah Wright are fascinating documents of Cold War political circumspection. In these letters, the correspondents cautiously come out of their political closets through the mention of various names in common (e.g., W.E.B. Du Bois, Shirley Graham, David Du Bois, Walter Lowenfels) proclaiming Left political sympathies in ways that did not reveal too much at once either to the letters' recipients—or any third party who might be reading the mail (Rosey Pool Papers, Moorland-Spingarn Research Center, Howard University, Box 82–1 Folders 6, 8, and 48, and Box 83–3, Folder 165).

14. Baraka, *The Autobiography of LeRoi Jones* (New York: Lawrence Hill, 1997), 134.

15. Baraka, *Autobiography*, 109–10.

16. Salaam, "Enriching the Paper Trail," 329.

17. Pauli Murray, "A Blueprint for First Class Citizenship," in *Reporting Civil Rights, Part One: American Journalism 1941–1963* (New York: Library Classics of America, 2003), 62–67.

18. Ekwueme Michael Thelwell, "The Professor and the Activists: A Memoir of Sterling Brown," *Massachusetts Review* 40: 4 (Winter 1999–2000): 617–38.

19. Author's interview with Muhammad Ahmad; author's interview with Michael Thelwell.

20. Kwame Ture (Stokely Carmichael) and Ekwueme Michael Thelwell, *Ready for Revolution: The Life and Struggles of Stokely Carmichael* (New York: Scribner, 2003), 86–95; Clayborne Carson, *In Struggle: SNCC and the Black Awakening of the 1960s* (Cambridge: Harvard University Press, 1981), 162.

21. Author's interview with Muhammad Ahmad; author's interview with Michael Thelwell.

22. For an example of this linking of the new and the old radicalisms written a little after the high-water mark of Black Arts/Black Power, see Killens, "The Artist and the Black University," 61–65.

23. For an account of the 1966 Fisk conference, see David Llorens, "Writers Converge on Fisk University," *Negro Digest* 15: 8 (June 1966): 54–68. For a brief description of the Hayden–Tolson debate at the conference, see Robert M. Farnsworth, Robert M. *Melvin B. Tolson, 1898–1966: Plain Talk and Poetic Prophecy* (Columbia: University of Missouri Press, 1984), 297–98.

24. For a short description of the 1967 Fisk conference, see "On the Conference Beat," *Negro Digest* 16: 9 (July 1967): 90–93.

25. Author's interview with Amiri Baraka; author's interview with Michael Thelwell; Thelwell, "The Professor and the Activists," 626–27. For the best account of the *Dasein* group and their work, see Aldon Nielsen, *Black Chant: Languages of African American Post-Modernism* (New York: Cambridge University Press, 1997), 59–77.

26. Author's interview with Michael Thelwell.

27. For accounts of Civil Rights and Black Power movements (and the difficulty of drawing a clear line between the two movements) in a number of small southern cities, often in the words of participants in those struggles, see Tom Dent, *Southern Journey* (New York: William Morrow & Company, 1996).

28. Eugene B. Redmond, *Drumvoices: The Mission of Afro-American Poetry: A Critical History* (Garden City: Anchor, 1976), 375–81.

29. Institute of the Black World, "Statement of Purpose and Program," in *New Black Voices: An Anthology of Contemporary Afro–American Literature*, ed. Abraham Chapman (New York: New American Library, 1972), 575–78.

30. For a short history of the inception and early days of the Institute of the Black World, see Stephen Ward, "'Scholarship in the Context of Struggle': Activist Intellectuals, the Institute of the Black World (IBW), and the Contours of the Black Power Radicalism," *Black Scholar* 31: 3–4 (Fall–Winter 2001): 42–53.

31. A. B. Spellman, "Letter from Atlanta," *Cricket* 3 (1969): 1–7; author's interview with A. B. Spellman, December 28, 2000, Washington, D.C.

32. Historian Robert Harris, Jr. recalls attending a meeting in John Henrik Clarke's apartment in New York City to discuss the creation of a new journal to replace *Black World* that helped lead to the founding of First World (Robert Harris, Jr., Comments, Modern Cultural Politics panel, Organization of American Historians annual meeting, Memphis, Tennessee, April 3, 2003).

33. For an account of the black theater scene and its limitations in Atlanta during the Black Arts period, see Barbara Molette, "Atlanta," *Black World* 22: 6 (April 1973): 88–92.

34. For an account of the forces leading to the formation and the decline of CAP and its role in establishing this Modern Black Convention Movement, see Komozi Woodard, *A Nation within a Nation: Amiri Baraka and Black Power Politics* (Chapel Hill: University of North Carolina Press, 1999), 219–54.

35. Author's interview with Ebon Dooley, August 16, 2001, Atlanta, Georgia; Adolph Reed, *Stirrings in the Jug: Black Politics in the Post-Segregation Era* (Minneapolis: University of Minnesota Press, 1999), 1–52.

RICK BENJAMIN

Mixed-up Medium: Kevin Young's Turn-of-the-Century American Triptych

Among contemporary poets, no one's more in tune to his diverse subjects or more mixed-up in both his craft and mass media than Kevin Young. He is a maker of old-school and of-the-moment modes and forms, a serious practitioner and technical innovator. Since 2001 Kevin Young has composed three volumes that not only offer up a new and rich blend of both ancestral and contemporary consciousnesses, but also a diverse and wide-ranging poetics that is this new century's *Montage*. Referential and reverential, equal parts throwback and visionary, Young's a hybrid of the known and new. In his long-book meditation on the artist Jean-Michel Basquiat, for example—*To Repel Ghosts* (2001)—he employs a version of Dante's terza rima and the hip-hop or pop artist's approach to archiving history. In *Black Maria* (2005), film noir meets mock-heroic couplets, a bittersweet coupling figured through film. In his third book, *jelly roll* (2003)—a National Book Award finalist—the blues form's stretched, in this case to joy and back. Even his first book, *Most Way Home*, a National Poetry Series winner in 1995, is an audibly lyrical meditation on lineage and cultural heritage. With his latest book, Young completes a sustained cultural critique through the lenses of major African American artists and art forms. Together, the three volumes mark the emergence of a major voice in American poetry.

From *American Poets in the 21st Century: The New Poetics*, pp. 193–209. Copyright © 2007 by Wesleyan University Press.

125

To Repel Ghosts is a major retrospective, a deep drop into American hell-realms: racism, consumerism, fame, and addiction. The book is presented as a series of "discs" that, while reminiscent of vinyl and CDs, are also more wild, unwieldy, and sustained versions of these musical wraps. Young's discs have two or three sides and countless songs of which to keep track, signaling extended listening of this one, prematurely ended, black artist's life.

"Campbell's Black Bean Soup," is just the first of hundreds of Young's plumbing, punning, stripped-down terza rimas:

> . . . Bartering work
>
> for horse, Basquiat churned
> out butter, signing each
> SAMO©. Sameold. Sambo's
>
> soup. How to sell out
> something bankrupt
> already[1]

This is Dante's stanza in more short-limbed, downbeated form, harboring at once the audible labors of a poem like Hayden's "Those Winter Sundays" and the jumpy play of Hopkins's language and sprung rhythms in a poem like "Pied Beauty." I reference a mid-twentieth-century American poet and nineteenth-century English poet deliberately, because every deft move of Kevin Young's suggests apprenticeship to both traditional and contemporary forms. Just as Hopkins bent and truncated the sonnet to his exuberant and quirky telling, so Young means to retune the thirteenth-century terza rima for a more headlong and plummeting twentieth-century descent.

It's a fast-paced, freestyle world we've stumbled into, and Young himself enters it in a first-line gallop, all trochees, followed by resonant downbeats. Slant- and off-rhymed, heavily stressed, no more than two or three beats per line, language here is commensurately stretched, pressed. The double duty of words like "lofty" and "sell out" and "bankrupt" testifies to both crass commercialism—embedded in the puns—and also to more valuable currencies, the duplicity and double entendres suggesting an alternately playful and edgy representation of the neo-pop cultural moment seen in retrospect:

> Basquiat stripped
> labels, opened & ate
> alphabets . . .

... he smacked
the very bottom, scraping
the uncanny, making

a tin thing sing.
  (*TRG* 5)

Getting under the conceptual frame for this artist means getting under the
skin: the cost of seeing through and living past "labels." The sound of bang-
ing pots, the poet's trochees and dactyls, eat up Dada's premises, leaving only
the sound, the song of "a tin thing": this Campbell's soup can's sentient. In
the rhymed and hard-driving closing can also be heard the insidious melody
of the quick fix, the promise of freedom through metamorphosis—but the
arch of this illusion of transcendence will be decidedly downward, toward
"the very bottom" of human experience.

And so ensues a kind of "portrait of the artist" from five "sides." Some
sides, like this first one, called "Bootlegs," are excavating, explicatory: they
cover Basquiat's time at the experimental City As School, his stint hawking
postcards for heroin on St. Marks, his early shows and collaborations. These
early poems more or less take for granted the knowledge that Basquiat was
addicted to heroin, that his graffiti tag, SAMO, stood for "same old shit," that
neo-pop in the hands of Warhol was the bright surface of a soup can.

But one of the great achievements of *To Repel Ghosts* is its persistent
historicizing: one comes out of the book considerably more educated about
Basquiat, his artistic and cultural milieu, about the perverse and myriad ways
America reifies race. As historical document, biography, as self- and other-
conscious meditation on the life of the black artist in America—on all these
levels, *To Repel Ghosts* succeeds brilliantly.

Young's wildly associative three-line riffs sound the strange, appropriat-
ing American arts establishment in which the young black artist has found
himself. Part virtuoso performance, part warning label, poems like "Dos
Cabezas" are songs toward setting the record straight:

... the gap
in Basquiat's teeth

What me worry? ...

Warhol with hand raised
pensing or perhaps
picking his nose ...

            the pair, returning
            to Andy's Factory,
            the canvas still wet

            as a kiss. A gift. Sold
            at auction their faces fetch
            five times the asking—

            feeding frenzy . . .
                (*TRG* 55)

Young's poem has all the pleasures of Dada/pop/late *beat*: *Mad* Magazine's
Alfred E. Neumann inhabits Basquiat's own gap-toothed smile long enough
to suggest the generational difference between "B" and Warhol; Warhol is
either deep in thought or "picking his nose." Art here is one person's gift
and another's fix. The lines skillfully sound the connoisseur-consumer's
appetite, high-bidders devouring at a gallop. Without explicitly saying so,
Young refers here to the fact that Basquiat provided Warhol with a second
wind; their collaborations on large canvases relied upon the younger artist's
energy and vision. The older, white artist, however, disproportionately prof-
ited from their convergences in the auctions that followed their two-headed
compositions. Friendship or exploitation? the poem asks.

   "Amateur Bout," the twenty-fourth and one of the longest of the twenty-
seven "songs" on this first side of disc 1 embodies and sounds all of the contradictions of the young black artist making art in the belly of a beast whose
appetite for new blood seems bottomless. Young's figuring of this embattled
terrain as a boxing match—punch-drunk, hyped-up prowess circumscribed
by a roped-off ring—is brilliantly rendered:

            Blood in his mouth
            this morning, high
            cotton, a prize

            fight—trying
            to beat this thing,
            breathe easy

            as money.
            THIS IS NOT
            IN PRAISE

OF POISON
ING MYSELF ...
   (*TRG* 57)

"High cotton" here is both in the mouth and speaks of the cotton field where slaves pick (off) the fashion statement someone else wears. Dante's stanza is put to great use, as Young demonstrates the purgatorial nature of this fight, fought against multiple opponents: the "poison" of Warhol's "strictly cash," art awash in money; any addiction—whether drug- or desire- or fame-induced—that throws its own hooks; "THE UGLY, FAT LIKE A PIG" art establishment and the *all-consuming* culture of which it is a spectacle or centerpiece, apple in its mouth. It's a setup, dehumanizing traps masquerading as riches. And this *consuming* bout with addiction, co-optation and commercialism is, to Young's perfectly pitched ear, all pop-punned, run-on:

He's off
like a bet—dime
bag, training

bag, punch
drunk & judy—
a hit—

THE CUSTOMER ...
       •

JUNK AND CIGARETTES
   (*TRG* 61)

Young's extraction of Basquiat's capitalized words from the canvas for integration into the language of his own poem is deft, connective: heroin and consumer culture are one. In Young, Basquiat has a loyal transcriber, a twenty-first-century interpreter of maladies for both the young, late twentieth-century black pop artist and contemporary poet.

Young easily and opportunistically borrows others' words to fill in blanks and for purposes of transition. Poems about the dropping of the atomic bomb on Hiroshima ("Gringo Pilot"), the Negro Leagues and the breaking of the color barrier ("Monarchs" and "3 Kinds of Fences"), and urban development ("Man-Made")—all based on paintings—are dropped in by way of representing more fully the range of Basquiat's catalogue. This is a country-sized canvas, a large-scale book of poems. "Gringo Pilot" is an early poem in *To*

Repel Ghosts that demonstrates Basquiat-Young's uncanny ability to sing the saddest stories of America while representing simultaneously the bomb-like quality of SAMO's© sorties as he tags the city:

> Trinity
>
> Test, Fat Man,
>
> Little Boy—unstable
> isotope, Boy—unstable
> core—
>
> Rita Hayworth taped
> to the bombshell. Exit
> Row. Do not write
>
> on the back. Write
> English with all capital
> letters. Keep form
>
> until departure from
> U.S.—deported, interred,
> Interrogated . . .
>   (*TRG* 21)

The "labeling" here is breathtaking, unexpected: Young black artist with a blond Mohawk ("English with all capital / letters" his tagging medium) renders as aircraft the heart of white America. "Little Boy"—with its picture of a bombshell pasted to the bombshell—renders sex and slogans as literal tags marking the imminent depopulation of Hiroshima. Like Basquiat, Kevin Young can't not make connections: deportation, internment, interrogation (race matters) the extraordinary marshaling of artlike energy in military projects like Trinity, identity of the perp hidden in a plane's black box.

When it comes to identities, *To Repel Ghosts* performs multiple acts of excavation. One of the best of these acts is side 2's twenty-two-page revisionist project on the boxer, Jack Johnson (29. Jack Johnson). Young's three-line stanzas are punctuated by statements from Du Bois, Booker T. Washington, Jack London, Miles Davis, among others. The effect is collage, crescendo, collapse; that is to say, all of the effects one might see also on Basquiat's canvas representing the same subject. Young charts the rise and fall of the artist-icon with a montage that reads like a history lesson, a cautionary tale, the boxer accounting for himself at the same time that others speak both for and against him. Segregating the icon from the iconography surrounding him, he finds the boxer's stance and pulls out all the stops. Lyrical and muscular, this telling goes the distance, fifteen rounds mixing first-person singular and secondhand accounts:

> That fight with Willard was a fix
> not a faceoff. Out of the ring
> three years, jonesing
> for the States, I struck a deal
> to beat the Mann
> Act—one taste of mat
>
> & I'd get
> let back home . .
> * * *
> Down, I counted too, blessings
> instead of bets. Stretched
> there on the canvas
>
> —a masterpiece—stripped
> of my title, primed
> a return to the States.
>
> Sated. Best
> believe I stood up
> Smiling,
>   (*TRG* 80–81)

Young underscores the hypocrisy, racism, and corruption informing this bout, while the voice of the now former heavyweight champion is a kind of chilling play of puns and double entendre. The great irony of "I struck a deal / to beat the Mann"; the relentless, downbeated punning in the verbs "down," "stretched," "stripped," "primed," and "saved"; the sound of both triumph and a sigh of relief in the words "Best / believe I stood up / smiling"—all testify eloquently for victory in defeat, for the willingness to play a game in order to get out of one. Young's own virtuoso performance here is in signaling fully the nature of Johnson's cultural disaffection and defection. I can only begin to hint at the myriad pleasures and pressures of this important poem. May these few lines serve as a call to reading!

The movement from the painterly, biographical *To Repel Ghosts* to the second part of Young's trilogy, *jelly roll*, is a "giant step" between idioms. *jelly roll* is loose and liberating, swinging between "songs" that sound, to use Young's own words from the epigraph poem, "Epithalamion," both "eagled" and "unsettled" states. This is "A Blues" that has neither the gravity nor density of the earlier book's three-line drops into Dante-like hell-realms. Instead, this book's idiom is so sensuous that, even when giving voice to suffering it wallows in a pleasurable languor just beneath pain's surface. A common practice in both *To Repel Ghosts* and *jelly roll* is "taking culture, both black and popular," in order to "make it sing" (*GS* 8). Young has said that he and other poets of his generation are apt to "find ancestors anywhere the ghost takes them," and in the blues form, of course, he has many predecessors.

With a few notable exceptions, *jelly roll* is a slow dance of couplets, a fluid back and forth of love lost and gained, dying or becoming. This "blues" is as much about pleasure as pain. Many of the earlier poems read like an Elizabethan sonnet sequence, celebrating boundlessness and abundance even as there is the implicit awareness, as in "Cakewalk," that these are transitory accumulations:

> Baby, you make
> me want
> to burn up all
> my pies . . .
>
> sink some peach
> cobbler. See, to me
>
> you are a Canada
> someplace north
>
> I have been, for years,
> headed & not
>
> known it . . .
>
> you are a found
>
> fallen thing—
> a freedom—not this red
>
> bloodhound ground—
>   (*JR* 7–8)

The sound of the blues is in the sharply stressed awareness of what we will "burn up" for love. There's no getting around the sensuality of Young's language, the almost visceral attraction to something that's both life-giving and destructive. And this kind of blues, of course, also charts a trajectory of creative progress and disintegration: language itself here—as in the self-conscious sonnet sequences of Sidney or Shakespeare—is the fuel as well as the hand that extinguishes. An early poem like "Siren" signals this doubling of desire and its singular expressions, whether heralding a new spark or a dying ember:

> On the fire throw
> another can of sterno
>
> that hiss is
> flame finding
>
> the wood wet . . .
>
> I mean, darling,
> to be an ABC
>
> extinguisher, kept
> handy, kitchened, a six-alarm
>
> APB . . .
> (*JR* 10)

Like what it describes, such language has the power to suffocate as well as suffuse; in the agile rhymes, in the alliterative and sprung rhythms, in the associative, quick-stepping thought is an undercurrent of "bad luck & / heart." What's carnal can't last.

   In the very next poem, "Rhythm & Blues," Young manages at once to surface the sound of emancipation, containment, and a self-conscious wistfulness:

> Through the wall
> I hear them
>
> again the couple—
> not fighting
> but doing
> the other thing—

> his cat-cries
> as if a trapped beast . . .
>
> her quiet—my own
> eavesdropped breath—
>   (JR 11)

This couple's contained in and circumscribed by their couplets, of course, the "trapped beast" still aspiring toward something surpassingly sacred: what's transcendent and transitory are one. And the poet, no mere interloper, also drops the breath of his own expression from the eaves, another fallen thing. Even first-person can't stay this tide, as in "Etude":

> I love making
> love most just
>
> after—adrift—
> the cries & sometime
>
> tears over, our strong
> swimming done—
>
> sheet wreck—
> mattress a life—
>
> boat, listing—
>   (JR 14)

The moment after lovemaking is a "sheet wreck," conceived here as the bed-boat about to go down. Despite the quick-stepping, tenderly associative riffs of this tongue, love's adrift. Yet so much of the first part of *jelly roll* is about love's spark, the fire, even if what fuels it is also what burns it up, as in "Song of Smoke":

> . . . you stir
> me like coal
>
> and for days smoulder.
> I am no more
>
> a Boy Scout and, besides,
> could never

put you out . . .
   (*JR* 46–47)

The second part of *jelly roll* is where Young enters more familiar blues terrain, love going and gone bad, the self hurt hard but still half-longing for what's been lost. Like the first and third parts of the book, this midsection is composed of thirty-some poems, most of which stick to Gwendolyn Brooks's epigraph at the outset: *You are the beautified half / Of a golden burr.* "Sorrow Song" hits just the right note:

   . . . on the subway
   home, her mouth still

   on my mouth
   like the gospel

   (thick as a cough
   or its syrup) hummed

   by a woman on the loud
   orange seat beside me.

   What else besides us
   is this? working

   down bone, a bright
   hymn—asking, asking.
      (*JR* 69)

I love the way the balanced choriamb, "thick as a cough," with its hard kiss of sound on each side, gives way to the softer anapest, "or its syrup" (malady muffled by cure) and that the woman humming on the subway is similarly almost free of stress (soft-stepping anapest followed by the almost inaudible pyrrhic foot and a closing iamb). That's the more harmonious sound at play here. But the rest is strongly stressed loss, as if the word "loud" sounds some kind of percussive cue. I count thirteen stresses in the last four lines; almost every word is a point of emphasis: the sadness of goodbye is the "working / down bone." And, make no mistake, it is heavy, hard work.

Young's flow, his style, his play with rhyme and sprung rhythms—these pronounced and audible inflections just under the form—are the sounds of our own contemporary musical-poetic cipher. This poet loves his elders but he's also of and in the moment. In *jelly roll* form's not fixed: this book is "A Blues," not *the* blues. And Young stretches the genre into places it hasn't been before. This is particularly evident in the third section of *jelly roll*, where the poet greets loss through an almost visionary lens. Love, gained and lost, stretches, conceives (of) possibilities that simply did not exist before. The first poem in this last section, "Envoy," reads like a defection from "business" as usual even as it affirms breathing into a new instrument:

> I quit. Resigned
> from your company
>
> entirely—I walk
> like paper. Short
>
> notice. Mama,
> boss lady, I'ma
>
> miss you—so too
> the trees. Time
>
> now to get down
> to brass, to this
>
> bidness—of breathing—
>   (*JR* 123)

This summing up, the dedicatory poem of the last section of the book, is also a beginning, signaling a new way of singing. Nothing unusual in the quitting: successive iambs sound the normative, everyday. What's striking are the heavy stresses: "miss you—so too / the trees. Time," sadness pressing, pent up, practically every word emphasized—*that* kind of missing. But the last sound, though equally short-limbed, is a different kind of breathing. "Now to get down"—well-balanced choriamb—is both an enjoinder to settle down to the "real" work and an urging to jam(b), to make something vibrant and energetic from the old "job" left behind. There is, to put it another way, an opportunity for spaciousness inside sadness to which the artist now turns. No accident that the last sound is another choriamb, balanced but still trailing off with an extra, muted syllable. A faltering utterance to be sure, but also the sound of something (*dash*) continuing. It's a Dickinsonian maneuver, both explosive and unfinished, a primer for reading the last fifty-plus pages of this "blues."

What follows are poems with titles like "Ramble," "Anthem," "Honky Tonk," "Saxophone Solo," "Slide Guitar,' "Plain Song," and "Lyre"—song types, instruments, voices, versions, that speak eloquently of loss's double edge. If the habit of heartbreak is like a chain gang, throwing it off can feel like finding freedom, as in "Anthem":

> ... the chain gang
>
> breaks rocks out
> of *habit*—*hunh*—does not
>
> look up to see
> one man—*hunh*—chains
>
> trailing—*hunh*—broken
> as the jailbird's
>
> wing, fleeing the field—
> back stripes—*hunh*—stars
>   (*JR* 130)

Young pays tribute to ancestors and genre—blues seeded and sung by others in cotton fields, in slavery and while incarcerated—while also breaking free of the conceptual frame of both the singers and their songs. So much of the breathing in this final section's toward "stars," toward a "sight" that "spirits into flame" ("Tacit"), disembodied "wind," ("Saxophone Solo") even though this blues remains grounded, embedded in tradition. Another way of saying this is that Young stays steeped in a blues idiom, while nevertheless falling into language that hasn't yet been heard, as in "Tacit":

> Even language
> leaves us—even the train ...
>
> ... the ants
>
> who my house invaded
> heading everywhere, hungry
>
> for what is not there.

Since you, honey,
my cupboards being bare . . .
    (*JR*, 131)

It's Rilke, in his third Sonnet to Orpheus, singing toward the emptiness
human suffering engenders. Nothing in the cupboards, but bareness still
offers something that ants find before they catch fire.

   A few poems later in "Deep Song," such inquiry is couched in terms of
self-immolation and salvation, dive and leap:

Belief is what
buries us—that

& the belief in belief . . .

plunge in
—the lungs . . .

high ledge
the leap—a breath

above the lip of the abandoned
quarry—belief . . .
    (*JR* 144)

Again, the almost gravitational pull here is toward what's earth-bound;
"belief" is the ground that claims us but also the "plunge," or counter-
movement, toward ecstatic leaps and depths. Young puts his faith in what's
most elusive, nearest places to which love and love lost take us. Pain as
both source and salve drives this book to its bittersweet closure. Col-
loquial, casual, these poems are nevertheless pleas for release from pain.
Shut down, all signs signaling "closed," yet open to the last, bitter sweet-
ness, as in "Rock":

I swing shut . . .

. . . get drunk on little
things . . .

. . . The rocking chair don't

by itself rock—
If only she

was here to tell me
shut up, quit

complaining, to kiss
my mouth closed.
      (*JR* 149)

The hard, alliterative sounds at the end of this poem ("quit," "complaining,"
"kiss," and "closed") are an audible dissonance, but they are also the lover's
soothing *shushes*, fingers to mouth, lip-locked end to querulousness on the
singer's part. What spurs this blues can also stop it more or less on a dime.
The suffering's deep but also, in a moment, mutable, subject to an almost
immediate turnaround. No wonder there's so much pleasure in the singing,
then, in the hearing.

      The last book in Young's important American trilogy, *Black Maria*, sus-
tains precisely this blues sound as well as its themes of love lost, departed and
gone bad, but film noir is its foregrounded stage. Also composed primarily
in couplets, the book moves in slow dance between private eye and femme
fatale, stepping languidly through conventional noir plotline: set-up, seduction, sleuthing, double-crossing, betrayal.

      In obvious ways, it's the same old story; the novelty is that this time it's
being told in verse. All the energy and sweep's in the language, in the agile,
associative riffs, the elaborate collocations and contexts of the detective, the
chanteuse, the femme fatale, and the private dick. Young has the genre down
cold, the types, their lingo, the fogs in which they, furtively, duplicitously
move. The effect is not quite so deep as in the earlier two volumes of the trilogy, but the surface play here's breathtakingly swift, supple:

in the deep end

I could not swim,

we kissed & my bow tie
turned a whirligig, lifted

me high among the trees
till I could see

how far I'd fall, that between us
air was all

we had left. My eyes oysters

pried open—
shucks.
    (*BM*, 176–77)

She wore red like a razor—
cut quite a figure . . .

dividing day
from night, there

from here. Where
I hoped to be is near

her & her
fragrant, flammable hair—
    (*BM* 12)

"The Hunch" gathers evidence audibly in terminal rhymes, springs rhythms like sudden surprises for the sleuth. The language is slippery, seductive, sure, perfectly pitched to its subject. I love the dropping onto the word "shucks" in the first poem. Nothing is quite as it sounds, which is to say it's more than that. Enjambments are extensions into new sensations and pleasures. All the suspense is poetic, as in, *what will he think up next?*

It's not surprising that technique is front and center here, that the stage-hand's craft, the elaborate effects and machinations of poetic noir, are obvious as studio sets. The self-conscious artifice that is both this book's sleight of hand and stock-in-trade suggest a virtuoso performer at the top of his game. But also under the weather: this atmosphere's thick as self-deception. Despite the trappings, poem noir cuts to the bone:

I'm tired of the city
telling me what it needs

isn't me—that trust is more
necessary to the picture

than I am. Pay
the man. Head outside

where the dark gathers round

fires built in the empty
barrel of the moon, men holding

their palms to its light
as if warmth . . .

. . . tonight I'll wander home
to sleep a few
hundred years & hope

her poison kiss might
slay me at last awake.
        (*BM* 154–55)

Lines like "that mist is more / necessary to the picture" are so pyrrhic and
understated because his presence now seems to mean so little! Later, the six
successive iambs of "a stone—tonight I'll wander home / to sleep a few," with
their comforting, familiar poetic rhythm, is disrupted by the unexpected and
rather jarring line drop on "hundred" (trochee simultaneously breaking the
beat and sounding the depths and length of this dull fatigue). Like the barrel
of fire, writing itself offers some kind of warmth and transient comfort. But
the poet's tired and this form, like elegy, won't ultimately heal or hold.

In all of Young's books, so much depends upon that familiar American
idiom that frames our history and that at once testifies to and witnesses in
its many voices, versions, and vernaculars: heartbreaking losses and betrayals;
unspeakably sweet stays against such experiences; deep repositories of exploitation and brutality; freedom, as it always is in America, a dream deferred, yet
also, perhaps, just around the bend; impermanence itself the promise of an
end to suffering (but also, of course, to joy)—a rich, complex, contradictory
idiom and legacy to be sure. The great achievement of Kevin Young's trilogy is
that it speaks to all of this. While his early twenty-first-century blues calls up,
pays tribute to, poets like Gwendolyn Brooks and Langston Hughes, as well
as countless singers and musicians; while his aspiration to capture his cultural
moment is reminiscent of Walt Whitman's stretch to document his day; while
his loose, freestyling language and syntax reverberate back to Clifton, Hayden,

Dickinson, and Hopkins even as they reach, wild and improvisational, toward the prophetic—while all of this is unmistakably true—when either entering or leaving a book by Kevin Young you are also in the presence of something unmistakably *new*. This work is a jam session in progress: Coltrane out on a limb for thirteen minutes with that familiar melody of "Favorite Things," but in a way you've never heard before, dropping finally, but only for a moment, on dogs barking and bees stinging. He's playing our song: set ariff by reading; hanging on the next note.

NOTES

1. Kevin Young, *To Repel Ghosts* (South Royalton, Vt.: Zoland Books, 2001), 5. Subsequent quotations from Young's work will be cited in the text using the following abbreviations: *TRG = To Repel Ghosts*, *JR = jelly Roll* (New York: Knopf, 2003); and BM = *Black Maria* (New York: Knopf, 2005).

BIBLIOGRAPHY

Books by Kevin Young
Black Maria. New York: Knopf, 2005.
Blues Poems (editor). New York: Everyman's Library/Knopf, 2003.
For the Confederate Dead. New York: Knopf, 2007.
Giant Step: The New Generation of African American Writers (editor). New York: Perennial/ HarperCollins, 2000.
jelly roll. New York: Knopf, 2003.
Most Way Home. Hanover, N.H.: Zoland Books, 2000; New York: Morrow/ Quill, 1995,
To Repel Ghosts. South Royalton, Vt.: Zoland Books, 2001.

Selected Prose
"The Black Psychic Hotline; or, The Future of African American Writing." Introduction to *Giant Steps: The New Generation of African American Writing*, edited by Kevin Young, 1–12. New York: Perennial/HarperCollins, 2000.
"One Big Thing: An Exchange." Dialogue with Adam Kirsch on Howard Nemerov and contemporary poetry. *Poetry* 183, no. 3 (December 2003).
"Responsible Delight." On the poet John Berryman. *Kenyon Review* (Spring 1999), 160–61.
"Six Uzbek Poems by Langston Hughes." *Callaloo* (Fall 2002).

Interviews
Callaloo. Interview with Charles Rowell. Emerging Male Writers issue (Winter 1997).
Indiana Review 23, no. 1 (Spring 2001).
Poets & Writers. "'A Short Distance to the Blues': Art Interview, and Conversation with Colson Whitehead." Vol. 31, no. 1 (January–February 2003).
Bookworm. Interview on National Public Radio, produced by KCRW in Los Angeles, September 2003.

Selected Criticism
Brouwer, Joseph. "Black Maria: Verse Noir." *New York Times Book Review* (May 22, 2001).
Caldwell, Heather. "Why Poetry Still Matters." *Town & Country* (July 2003): 47–49.

Dove, Rita. "Poet's Corner." Two poems from *Most Way Home*, discussed in *Washington Post Book World* (August 13, 2000).

Hirsch, Ed. "Poet's Corner." Article on *Blues Poems*. *Washington Post Book World* (February 1, 2004): 12.

Thomas, Lorenzo. Discussion of poems "Jack Johnson" and "Everywhere Is Out of Town." In *Extraordinary Afrocentric Modernism and 20th Century American Poetry*, edited by Charles Bernstein and Hank Lazer. Tuscaloosa: University of Alabama, 2000.

ANNETTE DEBO

Ophelia Speaks: Resurrecting Still Lives in Natasha Trethewey's Bellocq's Ophelia

In *Bellocq's Ophelia*, Natasha Trethewey gives voice to the African American sex workers living in New Orleans' Storyville, a legalized red-light district, in the early 1900s. This volume of poetry is based on photographs by Ernest J. Bellocq, a commercial photographer who took a remarkable series of photographs of women most likely working in Willie Piazza's or Lulu White's "octoroon" brothels. Trethewey creates a composite character as the volume's primary persona and uses her to envision the aspects of her life that transcend the written histories and recorded images. She is a conflation of many of Bellocq's subjects: the woman . . . who is reminiscent of John Everett Millais's *Ophelia*, a woman visiting a fellow sex worker dying from venereal disease, a scantily clad woman enjoying a drink of rye, a pensive woman formally dressed in pearls and feathers, a nude woman awkwardly arching her back. By naming her Ophelia, Trethewey participates in the tradition of recovering mythic female figures denied a voice, what Alicia Suskin Ostriker has called "revisionary mythmaking" (212). Like Gloria Naylor in *Mama Day*, Trethewey chooses Shakespeare's Ophelia to redeem. Instead of insanity and death, Trethewey's Ophelia is given a voice with which to recount lost American history. The poems think through the photographs, practicing Trethewey's idea quoted in the epigram that "if you look at a photograph, if you really study the gestures and expressions

From *African American Review* 42.2 (Summer 2008): pp. 201–14. Copyright © 2008 Annette Debo.

145

that the people have in the photograph, you could see the rest of their lives, everything that's to come." In doing so, the poetry considers the historical setting of southern African American women in the early twentieth century, working-class women's labor, and the act of looking.

The 2007 winner of the Pulitzer Prize for Poetry for her third book *Native Guard*, Trethewey is fulfilling the promise Trudier Harris and Opal J. Moore identified when they each included her in their compendia of rising women writers to watch in the twenty-first century (Harris 235; Moore 346–47). She has also received acclaim from Rita Dove, who chose Trethewey's first volume of poetry, *Domestic Work*, for the Cave Canem Prize in the first year it was awarded and who wrote the introduction for that collection, designating Trethewey "a young poet in full possession of her craft" (xii). As well as participating in Cave Canem, Trethewey is part of the Dark Room Collective, a community of poets including Sharon Strange, Thomas Sayers Ellis, Major Jackson, and Kevin Young, and her work is well represented in anthologies like Young's *Giant Steps: The New Generation of African American Writers*. Reviewers of all three of her volumes comment on the life she brings to historical photographs, her complex examination of racial identity, and the authenticity of her voice. Likewise, they praise the fluidity of her language, her intricate use of poetic forms, and the lyrical beauty of her verse. Reviewing *Bellocq's Ophelia* in some depth, Sarah Kennedy writes that "spare and elegant, *Bellocq's Ophelia* is not the tale of Storyville that American historians and popular culture have led us to see as its 'truth,' but that is much of Trethewey's point" (162). She comments particularly on Trethewey's usurpation of power as she gives Ophelia a camera of her own with which to capture her world. V. M. Kouidis is particularly interested in Trethewey's use of art and how art is complicit in Ophelia's victimization. Kouidis writes that "as genre criticism and as historiography, 'Ophelia' participates in the cultural and ethical criticism that has superseded French theory" (iii). Literary and art critics Debora Rindge and Anna Leahy explore the intertextuality between Trethewey's poetic narrative and Bellocq's photographs, examining in detail the relationships between poems and particular photographs (291–92). These scholars, and Trethewey herself in two in-depth interviews with Charles Henry Rowell and David Haney, have opened the critical discussion about her poetry, and this article is at the very beginning of the scholarly attention Trethewey will no doubt receive.[1]

In *Bellocq's Ophelia*, Trethewey creates a voice for the many women that Bellocq photographed in much the same way that other contemporary African American poets are reinterpreting American history. For example, in *M-A-C-N-O-L-I-A*, A. Van Jordan re-tells the life of MacNolia Cox from Akron, Ohio, who in 1936 won her district spelling bee and advanced to the national competition. As she continued to challenge her white opponents by spelling all her words correctly, the white judges dredged up "nemesis," a word suspiciously not on the approved list, to force her defeat. Similarly, Young revisions the career of boxing champion Jack Johnson in *To Repel Ghosts*. The heavyweight champion from 1908 to 1915, Johnson attracted white bigotry through his boxing prowess, his flashy, unapologetic lifestyle, and his marriages to white women. This impulse to reinvent figures in American history is shared by fiction writers, many of whom, like Toni Morrison, Charles Johnson, Sherley Anne Williams, and Edward P. Jones, are writing neo-slave narratives, which try more fully to grasp the slave experience than eighteenth- and nineteenth-century narratives were allowed by their white publishers. This convergence of so many authors involved in such similar projects of reinterpreting American history indicates a primary concern of this generation of writers.

Into historical memory and literary tradition, Trethewey restores the voices of Storyville women, what Rowell calls "inscriptive restoration" (1023; original italics). In an interview with Rowell, Trethewey explains her intentions:

> I think I've been concerned with what I have noticed to be the erasures of history for a very long time. Those stories often left to silence or oblivion, the gaps within the stories that we are told, both in the larger public historical records and in our family histories as well, the stories within families that people don't talk about, the things that are kept hushed. And so I've always been interested in those contentions between public and cultural memory, larger history and private or family memory and stories. And so I do seek to restore or to recover those subjugated narratives. (1023)[2]

In a different interview, this one with Haney, Trethewey describes her work as one of the layers in a cultural understanding of Ophelia. For Trethewey, the first layer is Millais's famous painting of a deadly passive Ophelia floating down the stream surrounded by flowers. In discussing this image, she comments, again demonstrating her empathy with the objectified image, "I know that the woman who posed for Millais died of pneumonia afterwards. So she just becomes a mention in history books, but he was the artist. He made this thing that's lasting" (28). The second layer is Bellocq's photograph, . . . *Hamlet's* Ophelia is the third layer in the cultural interpretation of Ophelia. Finally, Trethewey positions her Ophelia as the next layer: "So then there's the fourth layering, the next woman Ophelia, who is my character Ophelia, who actually can then speak where there has been no voice before" (Haney 28). In constructing this fourth layer, Trethewey chooses an image strikingly different from Millais's. This Ophelia, who has "in her face, a dare," stares back at the camera. Not only will her story now enter into history, but she also refuses the empty endings written by Shakespeare and painted by Millais. This Ophelia has agency, "her lips poised to open, to speak" (Trethewey, *Bellocq's* 3). She resists the many imposed frames with her determination to look back, and she opens her mouth to tell her own story, to become subject rather than object. Alone, this photograph tells only a story of possibilities with a subject frozen in time, forever about to speak. In her poetry, however, Trethewey, while unable fully to recover the unnamed and unacknowledged woman actually photographed by Bellocq, can create a possible narrative, rooted in the body of Bellocq's work and the few existing historical records.

The volume of poetry consists of five free-standing poems, fourteen "letter" poems constructing Ophelia's experiences for a loved confidante, and ten "diary" poems contemplating those same experiences. The opening poem, "Bellocq's Ophelia," initiates the complex connections between poetry, photography, and painting, and its narrator, whose story, though nonlinear, is nevertheless being told, constructs Ophelia who then tells her own story in the letter and diary-poem sequences. The second poem, "Letter Home," explains Ophelia's plight. Leaving behind a bleak future of domestic labor, she has moved to New Orleans to seek an office position. Unfortunately, no businesses are hiring, even when she experiments with passing; sex work, however, abounds. Life in a brothel is explained in the following poem, "Countess P—'s Advice for New Girls"; Ophelia has reached Storyville. In the letter and diary poems that follow, Ophelia explains her journey, and these poetic sequences reflect Ophelia's external and internal lives. The letter poems, which employ regular stanzas in a variety of lengths, are written to her friend and former teacher, Constance Wright.[3] Trethewey describes their changing forms as "an attempt to show the constantly changing self.... I almost felt like she was trying out different selves each time she wrote a letter to Constance" (Haney 24). These poems confide to Constance Ophelia's decision to work in Storyville in the face of imminent starvation and shape her difficult experiences for the eyes of a loved and concerned friend. More intimate are the diary poems, written in unrhymed sonnets. Trethewey chose a stricter form for this series because she hoped "to imply with the diary that there is perhaps some tiny little core of self that [Ophelia] didn't even realize she had" (Haney 24). These poems take readers further into Ophelia's life and her own burgeoning identity as a photographer. They interact with the letter poems in a similar fashion to Dove's *Thomas and Beulah*, in which Thomas's story, Beulah's story, and the timeline of American history quite differently represent the same events. Judith Kitchen comments that "there are many ways to tell a story, and Trethewey has chosen to give us Ophelia from several angles, almost as though the poet, too, were posing her" (1024). The final two freestanding poems, "Photograph of a Bawd Drinking Raleigh Rye" and "Vignette," both focus on the art of photography and the activity of looking.

In order to assess the historical setting of southern African American women in the early twentieth century, Bellocq's identity and the setting of Storyville are worth considering here, even though Bellocq's subjects, rather than he himself, are emphasized by Trethewey's poems. Trethewey has said that she "wasn't interested in [Bellocq's] story" because "we know much more about him than we know about the anonymous women that appeared in his photographs" (Rowell 1031). Nonetheless, understanding the context for Bellocq's photos is necessary to fully understand Trethewey's poetry because of its myriad historical references. In short, Bellocq was a commercial photographer who lived in New Orleans from 1873 to 1949. Because so few facts are decisively known about Bellocq—in 1973 John Szarkowski wrote that "our knowledge of E. J. Bellocq barely transcends the level of rumor" (*Looking* 68)—myths readily sprang up. Much of Bellocq's mystique can be traced to the compilation of interviews edited by Szarkowski and printed in the 1970 collection *E. J. Bellocq: Storyville Portraits*. These "interviews," based on actual interviews, hearsay, and creative editing, constructed the portrait of a "*hydrocephalic semi-dwarf*," fashioning New Orleans' own Toulouse-Lautrec (Szarkowski, Interviews 8; original italics). Further embellishment of Bellocq developed as he was mythologized in many texts. Most famously, Louis Malle's film *Pretty Baby* imagines Bellocq's life, in which he photographs the sex workers and eventually marries a very young girl, played by Brooke Shields. The documentary film *Storyville: The Naked Dance* uses Bellocq's photographs to illustrate its narrative line. In her novel *Storyville*, Lois Battle gives Bellocq a brief mention as she illuminates the complicated tangle of class, property, and sex in New Orleans. Similarly, Bellocq is a character in Michael Ondaatje's novel *Coming Through Slaughter* and Peter Everett's *Bellocq's Women*. Finally, in addition to inspiring Trethewey's poetry, Bellocq and his photographs inspired Brooke Bergan's volume of poetry *Storyville: A Hidden Mirror*, which includes "To Bellocq in Heaven" and endeavors to capture the many voices of Storyville.[4]

Recent research, however, has attempted to set the record straight. The most accurate published account of Bellocq's life is Rex Rose's "The Last Days of Ernest J. Bellocq." (Additional information about Bellocq was made public during a 1997 exhibit at the New Orleans Museum of Art, curated by Steven Maklansky, but has not yet been published.) Rose's Bellocq was an average man, standing about 5'6" in the prime of life, a bit more attractive than in other depictions of him, entirely sane with a penchant for flamboyant dress, professionally talented, and who rarely shared his Storyville plates with anyone. He grew up in a privileged French Creole family with one younger brother, Leo, who became a Jesuit priest. After completing a classical, parochial education, Bellocq began work at the wholesale firm in which his father worked. After a succession of jobs, he appears to have dedicated himself to photography after his mother's death in 1902. The family house, in which he remained, was located only one block from Storyville, providing him with easy access to the women he photographed, perhaps for profit (the photos may have been intended for advertising purposes) or for his own pleasure (Rose, "The Last" 14–21).

After his death, Bellocq's heir Leo probably found the Storyville plates in his apartment, but no documentation exists listing these items, which were by then illegal to possess. Antique shop owner Sal Ruiz bought the contents of Bellocq's apartment, later selling the Storyville plates to Larry Borenstein or Al Rose (there is some dispute). Borenstein, whom Maklansky describes as "quite the character and a dealer," had some prints made by Dan Leyrer, selling them for about $10 apiece. Many of these early prints ended up in the hands of Al Rose and are reprinted in his book about Storyville. In 1965, the plates sustained water damage from Hurricane Betsy, leaving substantial scarring inexistent in the early prints (Rex Rose, "The Last" 22–24). Photographer Lee Friedlander bought Bellocq's plates from Larry Borenstein in 1966, reprinted the plates, and helped publicize their artistry and existence, beginning with a major show at New York's Museum of Modern Art in 1970 (Friedlander 5).[5]

Storyville itself was created by the Story Ordinances in 1897 and dissolved in 1917 by the Navy, ostensibly to protect the morals of young men passing through New Orleans on their way to fight in World War I. Storyville encompassed about fifteen city blocks, from North Robertson Street to North Basin, and from Iberville Street to St. Louis Street (Al Rose 38, 72). The District was filled with opulent bordellos, shooting galleries, saloons, restaurants, cabarets offering the very best jazz and ragtime, small brothels, one-room cribs, and one church. By creating a vice district, New Orleans politicians hoped to separate the sex workers from the more respectable citizens, who ironically often owned property in the District or gained financially from it. In *The Great Southern Babylon*, Alecia P. Long points out how soon this district was formed after the *Plessy v. Ferguson* decision legalized racial segregation, timing which she claims was "no coincidence." She writes that "physical segregation was a popular solution to a range of social problems at the turn of the century, including the spread of disease, race relations, and prostitution" (103). Not only were the "lewd" women confined to the district—they could be arrested upon leaving it—but they were also separated by race within Storyville. According to Al Rose, the District was racially segregated ". . . in the sense that white and black prostitutes could not live or work in the same house and blacks were not permitted to patronize any of the mansions, even those staffed by black women or to consort with white women in even the lowest of cribs" (67). The sex workers plied their trade in houses that were anywhere from one-room "cribs," opening right onto the street and offering cut-rate prices, to the opulent Basin Street mansions which commanded impressive fees.

Storyville included a few houses that advertised their employees as octoroons, an antiquated term designating a person whose heritage is one-eighth African. The advertisements for Storyville marked the images of sex workers with a "W" for white, "C" for colored, and "Oct" for octoroon. When asked why he was certain that the women in Bellocq's photographs were indeed sex workers, especially since many of them are fully dressed, Friedlander replied that ". . . the wallpapers that appear in some of the photographs had been identified by contemporaries as having been in Mahogany Hall, one of the Storyville bordellos, run by a woman named Lulu White" (Malcolm 14).[6] An establishment employing only octoroon sex workers, Mahogany Hall boasted identifiable, exclusive wallpaper among its lavish furnishings. Thus, the women working in this prestigious house would have had African heritage, although on occasion white women did pass as octoroons in order to work there.

New Orleans has a long history of inequitable interracial sexual relationships, both the predatory relationships of white men buying light-skinned slaves for strictly sexual purposes and the more businesslike relationships between white men and free light-skinned women governed by legal contracts known as "plaçage," a system Floyd D. Cheung calls "a ritualized system of prostitution" (8). The nineteenth-century quadroon balls, according to Cheung, were a means of making light-skinned African American women available to white men as well as a way to deny them to African American men, who were banned from the balls by law. In the midst of this complex history, the term octoroon becomes more significant as an "eroticized descriptor" than a racial designation:

> Octoroons were supposedly refined and cultured, sophisticated and cosmopolitan, but their physiological make-up also promised something of the rapacious sexuality attributed to those with colored skin. Their sexuality was constrained, but not overridden, by their whiteness. Further, they could relate to white men in many of the same ways that refined white women could without the burden of passionlessness to regulate those encounters. Octoroons stood

astride the breaches in nineteenth-century sexual ideologies, a feat
that could only be managed by those who could claim to be two
kinds of women inside one body. (Long 206)

In the early twentieth century, the octoroon houses materially benefited
from this sexual fetish, as they could out-price their white competitors. It is
into this historical frame that Trethewey places Ophelia as she finds work
in an octoroon house.

Having established her interest in the work that women have done in the
past and continue to do in her first book of poetry *Domestic Work*, Trethewey
approaches the controversial occupation of sex work in *Bellocq's Ophelia*. She
situates Ophelia as a woman growing up in the post-Reconstruction South
with exceedingly limited occupational choices. The work that her culture
allowed a woman of her class and race to do was labor-intensive field and
domestic work: "laundry, flat irons and damp sheets, the bloom / of steam
before my face; or picking time, / hunchbacked in the field—a sea of cotton, /
white as oblivion" (20–21). Her own mother was broken by the cotton fields:
"her face sunken where she'd lost her teeth, / the 100 lb. sack dragging behind
her / like a bride's train" (24). If she stayed with her family, Ophelia risked
victimization at the hands of local white men. In fact, some poems hint that
Ophelia had already been raped by white men before she fled her home (13).
Ophelia was also constantly oppressed by the fear of lynching, which was
used to enforce the low social position of African Americans. Her mother too
had been victimized by white men, as Ophelia's absentee father was white.

With unusual perseverance, Ophelia managed to obtain a cursory education, despite the lack of books and materials in her one-room school. Her
confidante and former teacher, Constance, widened her vision of the world,
in part, by teaching geography. Constance shows Ophelia her location on
the globe and in the country, instilling in Ophelia a hunger to move beyond
the constraints of her limited life. Inspired by her teacher, Ophelia longs to
travel and eventually leaves home in hopes of bettering herself by obtaining a
position in an office, which would be accessible to her if she passed for white.
The poem "Letter Home," an epistolary poem to her family rather than to
Constance, chronicles her exhausted efforts to find such employment, even as
a white woman. Her carefully practiced standard English and good writing
skills are not sufficient to gain an office job: "no one needs a *girl*" (7). She also
worries that her effort to pass will be discovered, and, like many people who
passed, she is estranged from both racial worlds because she fears exposure.

Ophelia finally accepts the offer of Countess P— so that she can afford
to eat. She confides to Constance that, having come to the absolute end of
her own resources, she went to the Countess when "I had to leave my hotel,

and I am / as yet adjusting to my new life" (12). The Countess is based on two actual Storyville madams, Willie Piazza and Lulu White, who both ran octoroon houses. Al Rose, perhaps not the most exact historian, nonetheless offers a useful description of Piazza:

> Willie, herself, was one of the most cultured "landladies" New Orleans ever had, an octoroon fully at ease in the English, French, Spanish, Dutch, and even the Basque languages, and possibly also in Portuguese. Widely traveled, the "Countess," who of course had no hereditary claim to such a tide, wore a monocle, smoked Russian cigarettes in a two-foot ivory, gold, and diamond holder, and favored a diamond choker around her slim neck. In contrast to Lulu White, Piazza could easily have "passed" for white. She was truly a fashion leader of her time, and many respectable matrons of New Orleans' first families attended the annual opening days at the Fair Grounds racetrack with their dressmakers in tow, just to copy the outfits worn by Countess Willie and her girls. (52)

The Countess also had an extensive library, a lure for Ophelia, who revels in the wealth of books now available to her, in comparison to the dearth of materials in her more respectable childhood school. Also credited with a love for literature and music, Lulu White ran Mahogany Hall, "the most celebrated brothel in America," which boasted four stories, five parlors, fifteen bedrooms (each with a private bathroom offering hot and cold water), an elevator, and elegant furnishings (Al Rose 80–81). However, most details about these remarkable women are absent from the poetry, as are the more sordid aspects of their craft. Trethewey's volume is provocative in creating a desire to know Ophelia's story but is not sexually titillating. This excision continually focuses attention on Ophelia rather than Storyville, about which much information already exists.[7]

For Ophelia, sex work is not the career she sought, but other than field or domestic work, it is what is available to her. Because she works in a brothel, Ophelia can support herself, send money to her mother for false teeth and a well, and save enough money to move on eventually. Despite her sudden prosperity, however, she fears being subsumed by her economic choice; she guiltily wonders if perhaps somehow she is suited to this profession, indicating how significant work is in people's lives.

The sex industry is as much about theatricality as it is about sex, and in *Bellocq's Ophelia*, the act of looking is layered, circular, and reflexive. In Ophelia's profession, looking is perhaps even more significant than the physicality of sex, and everyone is looking. Bellocq himself is part of the poetry as he photographs Ophelia and various aspects of her life as a sex worker; when outside of the quarter, Ophelia is seen by a Storyville habitué and then photographed by the police; Ophelia tries to pass and the entire world looks at her deception; and finally, Ophelia is granted the agency to look at herself. These layers of looking are complicated by the racial and gender identity of each person looking and by the way in which people are trained to look at others.

The first layer is found in a poem tided "Bellocq" in Ophelia's diary poems, which introduce "Papá Bellocq," who pays only to photograph Ophelia (39). She can pose as she wishes, and he uses the contents of her room as props.[8] She says, "I try to pose as I think he would like—shy / at first, then bolder" (39). Thus begins Ophelia's initiation into the ritualized looking of photography. Theories about Bellocq's relationship with the women he photographed abound. Friedlander suggests that the women were relaxed and comfortable in the photographs, implying friendship with Bellocq (5). Susan Sontag remarks that in many of the photographs, "there is little doubt that posing is a game, and fun" (Introduction 8). Nan Goldin, a photographer herself, comments lengthily on the respect and care Bellocq shows for his subjects (91). Joseph L. Ruby even hints that the women might have been Bellocq's lovers. Alternatively, Joe Sanarens points out that Bellocq may simply have paid for their time (Szarkowski, Interviews 15). Maklansky observes that the women were pros and accustomed to being looked at; additionally, Bellocq may have been photographing them for illustrations in the Blue Book, a guidebook for out-of-town visitors that introduced them to the many activities available in Storyville. He also points out the likelihood of Bellocq instructing them in their poses, which mimic the "French postcards" and genre photos of the period. The poses lend themselves, after extensive cropping, to the conventional portraits found in photographs of Bellocq's own apartment.

Peculiarly, a number of Bellocq's original photographic plates have scratches over or near the models' faces. Bellocq left no explanation of the photographs nor of the scratches, so theories accounting for the scratches have proliferated. For many years, Leo was credited with having scratched the plates out of priestly moral outrage at their images. That theory seems unlikely, however, because he could easily have broken the fragile glass plates if indeed he was appalled. A second theory is that the scratches were made by Bellocq or one of his models to protect the models' identities because many sex workers went on to live reputable lives; however, this theory is discredited by the photographs of models wearing domino masks, which effectively hide their identity. Additionally, several of the models whose faces were scratched out in one photograph appear in other images intact. A third theory is that Bellocq scratched the plates himself shortly after developing them (for unknown personal reasons) but before the emulsion dried and hardened (Rex

Rose, "The Last" 9). Maklansky emphasizes, however, that it is possible even today to wet the aging emulsion and scratch the plates, so the scratches could have been made at any time. He adds that there is no discernable pattern for which images were scratched and which were left intact, which makes a rational explanation almost impossible. Alternatively, Sontag, Malcolm, and Goldin all suggest that the defacements, whatever their source, represent the violence against women that is so common, particularly in the sex industry (Sontag, Introduction 8; Malcolm 15; Goldin 91, 142).

Trethewey uses two of these theories in her poetry. First, in "Portrait #2," Ophelia is posing nude, concentrating on "how not to be exposed, though naked, how / to wear skin like a garment, seamless" (Trethewey, *Bellocq's* 42). While she is in this vulnerable position, Bellocq demonstrates just how fragile her position is as he scratches her image, creating "a scar" on her body: "showing me how easy it is / to shatter this image of myself" (42). Just as Bellocq can effortlessly deface an image, so do sex workers often die from violence and disease, their lives being as fragile as the glass negatives. Second, Trethewey returns to the issue of scratching the plates in "Disclosure," in which poem Bellocq scratches a plate when he is displeased with the image produced. Ophelia compares his technique of distorting an image with her own: "But I know / other ways to obscure a face—paint it / with rouge and powder, shades lighter than skin, / don a black velvet mask" (44). She emphasizes the performative nature of sex work, how she takes on other identities in order to be looked at and to protect the self she considers her own.

Relieved as she may be to have only modeling demanded of her by Bellocq, Ophelia knows she is the object, not the subject, of the photograph. In a photograph, many people, not just the customer, can look at her, so photography is in some ways even more invasive than a single customer. She also recognizes that only Bellocq will be recorded by their culture: "I'm not so foolish / that I don't know this photograph *we* make / will bear the stamp of his name, not mine" (Trethewey, *Bellocq's* 39). Maklansky believes that Bellocq may have been taking the photographs for use, after substantial cropping, in advertising the brothel in a Blue Book. In the poem "Blue Book," Ophelia poses in a fancy gown and looks away "to appear / demure" (40). The Countess markets her as "'*Violet,' a fair-skinned beauty, recites / poetry and soliloquies; nightly / she performs her tableau vivant, becomes / a living statue, an object of art*—" (40; original italics). This advertisement constructs her as a highly cultured person, one with whom upper-class men would have much in common. Ophelia is also positioned to contrast to the crass nature of the sexual circuses performed nightly by the women working for Emma Johnson, an infamous Storyville figure.[9] Additionally, not only is Ophelia renamed and given highly cultured attributes, she is presented as performing a *tableau vivant*, a formalized silent spectacle in which Ophelia remains motionless, striking a pose from a classical painting. The customers watching can construct her into anything that they wish; it is her job to become an actor in their desires, an acute accentuation of Laura Mulvey's well known theory of the gaze.

In her existence as a sex worker, Ophelia embodies what Mulvey has called "looked-at-ness" (19). Bellocq pays to photograph her for his own plea-sure and perhaps profit; she nightly performs the *tableau vivant* to entice cus-tomers to cast her in their fantasies; some customers pay simply to look at her nude; and she becomes an octoroon spectacle for the customers determined to identify her African traits. The treatment of her as a spectacle is even more accentuated when, to initiate her into the trade, she is paraded before onlook-ers and then auctioned, reminiscent of the none-too-distant slave auctions, especially those of light-skinned "fancy girls."[10] Furthermore, in the free-standing poem "Photograph of a Bawd Drinking Raleigh Rye" (based on a distinctive photograph of a woman wearing striped stockings), Trethewey forces readers to enact what Mulvey describes as she directs the gaze toward the woman's feet and up her body:

> The glass in her hand is the only thing moving—
> too fast for the camera—caught in the blur of motion.
>
> She raises it toasting, perhaps, the viewer you become
> taking her in—your eyes starting low, at her feet,
>
> and following those striped stockings like roads,
> traveling the length of her calves and thighs. Up then,
>
> to the fringed scarf draping her breasts, the heart
> locket, her bare shoulder and the patch of dark hair
>
> beneath her arm, the round innocence of her cheeks
> and Gibson-girl hair.... (*Bellocq's* 34)

In exploring the nature of photography, Sontag writes, "To photograph is to appropriate the thing photographed" (*On* 4). These poems enshrine Ophelia in her role of being looked at from her toes upward.

John Berger's theories on how nude women are looked at in paintings are also applicable to Ophelia because, despite her sense of "looked-at-ness," she refuses to passively accept the many stares. Ophelia, especially through the *tableau vivant*, is looked at the way a painting is looked at. Through the tradition of European painting, Berger demonstrates how "the subject (a woman) is aware of being seen by a spectator" (49). Berger also argues, however, that that tradition begins to change in modern art. Berger compares Titian's *The Venus of Urbino*, in which the nude female subject demurely turns her head in acquiescence to the viewer's right to look, to Manet's *Olympia*. Manet's painting of a well known sex worker reclining in much the same position as Titian's figure gives no such acquiescence to the audience's right to look; Olympia looks squarely at the viewer. "One sees a woman, cast in the traditional role, beginning to question that role, somewhat defiantly," claims Berger (63). Janet Malcolm concurs and directly extends this analysis to Bellocq's work:

> As Manet's *Olympia* shocked viewers at the Salon of 1865 because instead of a rosy, complaisant nymph rising from the waves surrounded by cherubs, it showed a pale, self-assured prostitute lying on her unmade bed attended by a black maid and cat, so do Bellocq's nudes astonish us in the way they diverge from the conventions by which nude photography—of both the dirty and arty variety—was ruled in its day. (12)

Likewise, Trethewey's Ophelia unashamedly stares back at the audience. She forces recognition from her audience, shifting herself away from the position of simply being consumed. Instead, although exposed, she claims agency and places the audience in the conscious position of the voyeur. She knows that we are looking, and we are forced to recognize that knowledge, giving her the upper hand in the situation.

Another person who looks at Ophelia is her father, whom Trethewey likens to Bellocq. Her unnamed father, the sole identity of "white man" being enough to define him, bequeathed to Ophelia her troubled name, and shapes her by his demands and his absences. He is clearly a man of a higher social class because Ophelia is taught, as a child, to "curtsy and be still / so that I might please a white man, my father" (Trethewey, *Bellocq's* 20). During his occasional visits, which Ophelia feared, she longed for his approval—were her fingernails, ears, and teeth clean, could she differentiate between "lay" and "lie," was she more like him than her mother—and she learned early to mold her face to fit his desires in the same way that she ingested arsenic to whiten her skin (20).[11] She "wanted him to like me, think me smart, / a delicate colored girl—not the wild / pickaninny roaming the fields, barefoot" (38). Her cursory memories of this father have left no visual image in her mind, and because he is uncomfortably like her customers in his demands of her and his use of her mother, she fears that he might someday appear unrecognized in her current life, "both customer and father" (38).

Besides Bellocq, the customers, and her father, Ophelia is looked at by the police. In a letter poem, "October 1911," Ophelia dresses in proper clothes like "a club woman" (Trethewey, *Bellocq's* 28) and leaves the Quarter to visit a sick colleague dying of venereal disease. Upon leaving, Ophelia is recognized by a customer, who, instead of being embarrassed by his familiarity with her professional life, is incensed that she has left the bounds of Storyville. Once identified as a "lewd" woman, Ophelia is arrested and "suffered / indecencies" (29). She is probably beaten, very likely raped, and apparently painted (a scarlet red perhaps) to remind her of her social position and her physical limits in New Orleans culture. The police also take her photo, and she leaves behind a mug shot showing "paint" smeared on my face, my hair / loosed and wild—a doppelgänger / whose face I loathe but must confront" (29). This grim photograph too appropriates Ophelia's image, this time for the official business of keeping lewd women away from the neighborhoods of their customers.

The next layer of looking is that of the New Orleans community, black and white, who look for racial markings when Ophelia passes for white and when she does not. In "January 1912," a letter poem to Constance, Ophelia reveals her very light skin: "I think often of our unlikely meeting / your first day in our classroom—how / you mistook me for white" (Trethewey, *Bellocq's* 31). After gaining a basic education and standardizing her spoken English, Ophelia goes to New Orleans to improve her employment options. In order to obtain a position in a business, she decides to pass for white, but she constantly fears that she will be found out despite her fair skin. Choosing a white identity sits uncomfortably upon Ophelia. She watches passersby, feels their glances, and wonders how they identify her racially. Naturally, she worries that her African blood will be identified because she would then be excluded from all of the office jobs. In ironic contrast, after she begins employment as a sex worker, customers are obsessed with finding markers of her African heritage in her. The exoticism that the white customers are willing to pay for must exhibit itself in some way to mark Ophelia as other than white: "telltale / half-moons in our fingernails, / a bluish tint beneath the skin" (26). A particularly offensive customer inspects Ophelia for marks of racial identity, and she sees herself in his monocle: "I looked away from my reflection—/ small and distorted—in his lens" (26). These verses highlight the constructed nature of race and how the way people look at others aids in that construction.

The final, and finally liberating, viewer is Ophelia herself. In "February 1911," Ophelia remembers looking at herself when she is thirteen and able to appreciate how her body is maturing. The poem immediately juxtaposes her own looking with a white man's looking at her youthful figure and "pinching / the tiny buds of my new breasts" (Trethewey, *Bellocq's* 18), indicating that already her body is looked at. Her response, however, is to look beyond that place for an escape route to self-emancipation. Because she is looked at by this man, Bellocq, her customers, the police, and the community, Ophelia looks back. And unlike Millais's *Ophelia* and Titian's *The Venus of Urbino*, but more akin to Manet's *Olympia*, Trethewey's Ophelia looks back at us, challenging the viewer's right to purchase the representation of a person in order to consume it. As Kennedy observes, "readers lured by sexual description . . . may find themselves implicated in the objectifying gaze that has failed to see that the subject of this book is gazing back" (162–63).

Recognizing the power available in photographing images, Ophelia purchases a camera herself and, in addition to posing for Bellocq, learns techniques from him. She is most interested in the transformative power available in photography: "I've learned to keep / my face behind the camera, my lens aimed / at a dream of my own making" (Trethewey, *Bellocq's* 44). For example, she photographs a cardinal, and her photograph captures the bird's flight but chooses not to include the ground he has left, which is covered with "garbage, / rats licking the insides of broken eggs" (44). As a photographer, she suddenly notices the angles in the world around her and recognizes how "the camera can dissect / the body." Ophelia is drawn to "what shines," which Trethewey attaches to alchemy, the changing of dross into gold. The camera can do that also: it can "capture[e] / the sparkle of plain dust floating on air" (27), and it can transform Ophelia.

Ophelia learns Bellocq's craft: how to use light to capture that sparkle, how to position props, and how to compose scenes. During a session in which she is posing, she comments on what photographs present and what they hide. For example, in a photograph of her, her body and particular props are included, but the photographs cannot capture the more elusive aspects of her reality: the silverfish, nocturnal household pests living in the walls, and "the yellow tint of a faded bruise" (Trethewey, *Bellocq's* 43). Similarly, in a hospital photograph, two women, one well and one sick, are pictured. Bellocq has positioned them so that, according to Ophelia, the sick one represents what the healthy woman "*might become.*" Furthermore, beyond the sick woman is a door, "and beyond that door, / *what you cannot see,*" ostensibly death (28). The photograph shows the progression of one woman from healthy to ill to dead, the logical progression of many women who acquire sexually transmitted diseases, a common consequence of employment as a sex worker. The photograph offers this insight through its framing, implications, and omissions. As a photographer herself, Ophelia writes Constance that she hopes to photograph her, and she describes Constance in the stance she remembers her best, as a teacher turning from the board, looking at Ophelia. This image represents Constance for Ophelia rather than Constance's own reality, but it most significantly represents Ophelia outside of the frame as she would prefer to be, a student rather than a sex worker. Once in a position of power as a photographer, Ophelia focuses on a positive element in her past to represent herself.

Six months after buying her camera and having found power in capturing images herself, Ophelia escapes Storyville, heading west. Her final letter poem to Constance, "March 1912," includes the epigraph "*Postcard, en route westward*," and its content is that of transformation. In a renga, a series of linked haiku stanzas and a form which connects Trethewey to poets like Sonia Sanchez, Ophelia describes the coming of spring and how she "feel[s] what trees must—/ budding, green sheaths splitting—skin / that no longer fits" (33).[12] The springtime images of new life bursting forth perhaps indicate that Ophelia has left her life as a sex worker behind in Storyville and that she can choose a skin that fits better. Her diary entry of the same date, titled "*(Self) Portrait*," chronicles her earlier departure from her childhood home, an escape that offered new opportunities but at an unexpected cost. However, she has gained some measure of self-determination through her work in Storyville and as a photographer. Her earnings from Storyville allow her to move on, and instead of being photographed, she now photographs herself and her world. The camera's lens, capped and unable to take a photograph, reflects her "own clear eye" back to her (46); she has agency over her image now.

Bellocq's Ophelia ends with the poem "Vignette," based on a photograph of a woman wearing her best dress, laced with pearls, and a fur stole—the photograph which graces the cover of Trethewey's volume. Her hair carefully coiffed, the woman looks beyond the camera, which seemingly has caught her in an unguarded moment. Like Janet Malcolm, Trethewey calls this image a "decisive moment," which Malcolm defines as "when the contingent and the willed fuse in a kind of thunderclap" (14). The term is borrowed from Henri Cartier-Bresson, whose 1952 book *The Decisive Moment* showcases many such moments in photography. In his epigraph, Cartier-Bresson quoted seventeenth-century Cardinal de Retz's statement, "*Il n'y a rien en ce monde qui n'ait un moment decisive*," which translates as "There is nothing in this world that does not have a decisive moment." This photograph, then, is Ophelia's decisive moment. As Bellocq sets up the photograph, he entertains Ophelia with tales of a visiting circus, leading her thoughts to how, as a child, she saw a contortionist perform. Her thoughts, straying as she poses, then equate her own life to that of the contortionist:

> She thinks of her own shallow breath—her
> back straining the stays of a bustier,
> the weight of a body pressing her down. (47)

That connection allows the realization that life as a sex worker, while financially remunerative, will distort her further with every passing year. She will find the contortionist's role increasingly difficult. Perhaps this realization leads her to her risky decision to head west, into more uncertainty. In this decisive moment, Ophelia chooses a future, hopefully one in which she determines her position as a subject rather than an image:

> Imagine her a moment later—after
> the flash, blinded—stepping out
> of the frame, wide-eyed, into her life. (48)

NOTES

1. For additional reviews of *Bellocq's Ophelia*, see Campo, Dusseau, Kitchen, and Oktenberg.

2. See Haney for a similar answer (21).

3. Besides the obvious symbolism for a woman who is constant and right, the name Constance is shared with Constance Sullivan, editor of a collection of nude photography. Her volume briefly discusses Bellocq's work and reproduces three of his photographs.

4. Bergan's 1994 book may have been an inspiration for Trethewey's poetry. It offers a bibliography, listing many sources that influenced Trethewey's poetry as well.

5. Al Rose also includes information on Bellocq (59–60), but Rex Rose's research appears more accurate.

6. Maklansky pointed out that it is possible that not all of the women photographed were sex workers.

7. A notable absence from the poetry is the presence of jazz. Many famous jazz musicians, such as Jelly Roll Morton, learned their craft in the brothels while providing entertainment for the customers.

8. In reality, the women may have chosen their poses (although many seem similar and staged), but Bellocq did provide props. Rex Rose notes that "Bellocq draped the same locket around the necks of many of his sitters. Often he pushed heavy couches in front of locked doors during photo shoots in obsessive attempts at privacy" ("Welcome" 10). After Bellocq's death, a locket was listed in the contents of his safe deposit box, which may have been the locket used in the photographs (Maklansky).

9. See Al Rose for information on Emma Johnson (50–52).

10. Roach explores the intersections of sexuality and racial identity in the spectacle of the slave auctions, particularly in light-skinned "fancy-girl" auctions, in which "the sale of relatively well-educated and relatively white women into sexual bondage raised the erotic stakes" in a distinctly pornographic display (215).

11. Before writing *Bellocq's Ophelia*, Trethewey conducted extensive research. She comments that "one particular detail that I took from a historical document, from a letter in an archive, is the use of arsenic. One prostitute describes using it to stay pale, to be whiter" (Rowell 1029).

12. For Sanchez's use of haiku form, see *I've Been a Woman*, *Under a Soprano Sky*, *Wounded in the House of a Friend*, and *Like the Singing Coming Off the Drums*.

WORKS CITED

Battle, Lois. *Storyville*. New York: Viking, 1993.

Bellocq, E. J. *Bellocq: Photographs from Storyville, The Red-Light District of New Orleans*. New York: Random House, 1996.

———. *E. J. Bellocq: Storyville Portraits: Photographs from the New Orleans Red-Light District, circa 1912*. New York: Museum of Modern Art, 1970.

Bergan, Brooke. *Storyville: A Hidden Mirror*. Wakefield, RI: Asphodel P, 1994.

Berger, John. *Ways of Seeing*. New York: Viking, 1973.

Campo, Rafael. "Domestic Work/Bellocq's Ophelia/The Paintings of Our Lives/Days of Wonder." *Prairie Schooner* 77.4 (Winter 2003): 181–85.

Cartier-Bresson, Henri. *The Decisive Moment*. New York: Simon & Schuster, 1952.

Cheung, Floyd D. "Les Cenelles and Quadroon Balls: 'Hidden Transcripts' of Resistance and Domination in New Orleans, 1803–1845." *Southern Literary Journal* 29.2 (Spring 1997): 5–16.

Dove, Rita. Introduction. *Domestic Work*. By Natasha Trethewey. Saint Paul MN: Graywolf P, 2000. xi–xii.

———. *Thomas and Beulah*. Pittsburgh: Carnegie-Mellon UP, 1986.

Dusseau, Melanie. Rev. of *Bellocq's Ophelia*, by Natasha Trethewey. *Crab Orchard Review* 8.1 (Winter/ Spring 2002): 266–68.

Everett, Peter. *Bellocq's Women*. London: Random House, 2001.

Friedlander, Lee. Preface. Bellocq, *Bellocq: Photographs* 5.

Goldin, Nan. "Bellocq Epoque." *Artforum* 36.9 (May 1997): 89–91, 142.

Haney, David. "A Conversation with Natasha Trethewey." *Cold Mountain Review* 33.1 (Fall 2004): 19–34.

Harris, Trudier. "Greeting the New Century With a Different Kind of Magic: An Introduction to Emerging Women Writers." *Callaloo* 19.2 (Spring 1996): 232–38.

Johnson, Charles. *Middle Passage*. New York: Simon & Schuster, 1990.

Jones, Edward P. *The Known World*. New York: Harper Collins, 2003.

Jordan, A. Van. *M-A-C-N-O-L-I-A*. New York: Norton, 2004.

Kennedy, Sarah. Rev. of *Bellocq's Ophelia*, by Natasha Trethewey. *Shenandoah* 52.2 (Summer 2002): 160–63.

Kitchen, Judith. "Interlude." *Georgia Review* 56.4 (Winter 2002): 1011–26.

Kouidis, V. M. "Editors' Comment (Women and the Gaze, Remarks Concerning Gabriele Munter, Natasha Trethewey, Maurice Blanchot, and Edith Wharton)." *Southern Humanities Review* 33.3 (Summer 1999): ii–iv.

Long, Alecia P. *The Great Southern Babylon*. Baton Rouge: Louisiana State UP, 2004.

Maklansky, Steven, Assistant Director for Art, New Orleans Museum of Art. Telephone interview. 7 Mar. 2006.

Malcolm, Janet. "The Real Thing." *New York Review of Books* 44.1 (9 Jan. 1997): 12, 14–16.

Morrison, Toni. *Beloved*. New York: Plume, 1987.

Moore, Opal J. "Enter, the Tribe of Woman." *Callaloo* 19.2 (Spring 1996): 340–47.

Mulvey, Laura. *Visual and Other Pleasures*. Indianapolis: Indiana UP, 1989.

Naylor, Gloria. *Mama Day*. New York: Vintage, 1988.

Oktenberg, Adrian. "New blues, old photos." *Women's Review of Books* 21.1 (October 2003): 20–21.

Ondaatje, Michael. *Coming Through Slaughter.* New York: Norton, 1976.

Ostriker, Alicia Suskin. *Stealing the Language: The Emergence of Women's Poetry in America.* Boston: Beacon P, 1986.

Petty, Jill. "An Interview with Natasha Trethewey." *Callaloo* 19.2 (Spring 1996) 364–75.

Pretty Baby. Dir. Louis Malle. Perf. Brooke Shields, Keith Carradine, Susan Sarandon. Paramount, 1978.

Rindge, Debora, and Anna Leahy. "'Become What You Must': Trethewey's Poems and Bellocq's Photographs." *English Language Notes* 44.2 (Fall/Winter 2006): 291–305.

Roach, Joseph. *Cities of the Dead: Circum-Atlantic Performance.* New York: Columbia UP, 1996.

Rose, Al. *Storyville, New Orleans.* Tuscaloosa: U of Alabama P, 1974.

Rose, Rex. "The Last Days of Ernest J. Bellocq." *Exquisite Corpse: Journal of Letters and Life* 10 (Fall/Winter 2001/2002). 30 Aug. 2005. <http://www.corpse.org/archives/issue_10/gallery/bellocqindex.htm>.

———. "Welcome Home E. J. Bellocq." *Arts Quarterly* 18.2 (July/August/September 1996): 10–11.

Rowell, Charles Henry. "Inscriptive Restorations: An Interview with Natasha Trethewey." *Callaloo* 27.4 (Fall 2004): 1022–34.

Ruby, Joseph L. "Bellocq's Women." *New York Review of Books* 44.4 (6 Mar. 1997): 13 pars. 23 Aug. 2005. <http://www.nybooks.com/articles/1257>.

Sanchez, Sonia. *I've Been a Woman: New and Selected Poems.* Sausalito, CA: Black Scholar P, 1978.

———. *Like the Singing Coming Off the Drums.* Boston: Beacon P, 1998.

———. *Under a Soprano Sky.* Trenton, NJ: Africa World P, 1987.

———. *Wounded in the House of a Friend.* Boston: Beacon P, 1995.

Sontag, Susan. Introduction. Bellocq, *Bellocq: Photographs* 7–8.

———. *On Photography.* New York: Farrar, Straus, Giroux, 1973.

Storyville: The Naked Dance. Prod. Anne O. Craig and Maia Harris. Shanachie, 1997.

Sullivan, Constance. *Nude Photographs 1850–1980.* New York: Harper & Row, 1980.

Szarkowski, John, ed. Interviews. *E. J. Bellocq: Storyville Portraits* 3–18.

———. *Looking at Photographs.* New York: The Museum of Modern Art, 1973.

Trethewey, Natasha. *Bellocq's Ophelia.* Saint Paul MN: Graywolf P, 2002.

———. *Domestic Work.* Saint Paul, MN: Graywolf P, 2000.

———. *Native Guard.* New York: Houghton Mifflin, 2006.

Williams, Sherley Anne. *Dessa Rose.* New York: Harper Collins, 1986.

Young, Kevin, ed. *Giant Steps: The New Generation of African American Writers.* New York: Perennial, 2000.

———. *To Repel Ghosts: The Remix.* New York: Knopf, 2005.

Chronology

1952	*Invisible Man* by Ralph Ellison wins National Book Award.
1954	Supreme Court rules public school segregation unconstitutional in *Brown vs. Board of Education.*
1955	Emmett Till lynched by white mob in Mississippi; Rosa Parks refuses to give up her bus seat in Birmingham, Alabama.
1957	SCLC organized with Martin Luther King Jr. as president; public schools in Little Rock, Arkansas ordered to end segregation; integration action assisted by federal troops.
1959	Lorraine Hansberry's *A Raisin in the Sun* becomes first work by an African-American playwright to win Best Play of the Year award from the New York Drama Critics.
1960	Lunch counter sit-ins begin in Greensboro, North Carolina; Civil Rights Act of 1960 signed by President Eisenhower; Student Nonviolent Coordinating Committee (SNCC) founded in Atlanta.
1961	CORE Freedom Rides to enforce desegregation begin in the South.
1961	Amiri Baraka's *Preface to a Twenty Volume Suicide Note.*
1962	Efforts to enroll African American student James H. Meredith at the University of Mississippi requires assistance of 12,000 federal troops.

1963   Two hundred thousand people join the March on Washington to hear Martin Luther King's "I Have a Dream" speech.

1964   Malcolm X founds the Organization of Afro-American Unity; in an action known as Freedom Summer, students from the North join students from the South to register blacks to vote in the southern states; President Johnson signs the 1964 Civil Rights bill.

1964   Amiri Baraka's *Dutchman and the Slave* and *The Dead Lecturer*.

1965   Malcolm X assassinated in NYC; civil rights workers stage a five-day march from Selma to Montgomery, Alabama; Voting Rights Bill passes in the Senate; riots break out in the Watts section of Los Angeles.

1965   Amiri Baraka's *The System of Dante's Hell*.

1966   "Black Power" slogan enters the language, instantly becomes controversial.

1967   Ishmael Reed: *The Free-lance Pallbearers*; Jay Wright: *Death as History*.

1968   Martin Luter King Jr. assassinated in Memphis, Tennessee; Gwendolyn Brooks becomes first poet laureate of Illinois.

1968   Audre Lorde: *The First Cities*; Alice Walker: *Once: Poems*; Nikki Giovanni: *Black Judgment*; Mari Evans: *Where Is All the Music?*; June Jordan: *Who Look at Me*.

1969   Amiri Baraka: *Black Magic*; Ishmael Reed: *Yellow Back Radio Broke-Down*; Sonia Sanchez: *Homecoming*; Lucille Clifton: *Good Times*; Carolyn Rodgers: *Songs of a Blackbird*; Raymond R. Patterson: *26 Ways of Looking at a Black Man, and other Poems*.

1970   Amiri Baraka: *It's Nation Time* and *In Our Terribleness*; Audre Lorde: *Cables to Rage*; Nikki Giovanni: *Black Feeling, Black Talk and Re: Creation*; Michael S. Harper: *Dear John, Dear Coltrane*; Lucille Clifton: *Good Times and Some of the Days of Everett Anderson and The Black BC's*; Mari Evans: *I Am a Black Woman*; June Jordan: *His Own Where*.

1971   Ishmael Reed: *catechism of d neoamerican hoodoo church*; Maya Angelou: *Just Give Me a Cool Drink of Water 'Fore I Diiie*; *It's a New Day: Poems for Young Brothas and Sistuhs*; *Everett Anderson's Christmas Coming* and *Everett Anderson's Year*; Jay

Wright: *The Homecoming Singer*; Mukhtarr Mustapha: *Thorns and Thistles*.

1972   Amiri Baraka: *Spirit Reach*; Ishmael Reed: *Conjure: Selected Poems, 1963–1970; Mumbo Jumbo*; Alice Walker: Five Poems; Nikki Giovanni: *My House*; Michael S. Harper: *History as Apple Tree*; Lucille Clifton: *Good News about the Earth*; Conrad Kent Rivers: *The Wright Poems*; Ebele Oseye: *A Feast of Fools*; Ray Durem: *Take No Prisoners*.

1972   President Richard Nixon publicly opposes busing as a means of school integration; Shirley Chisholm runs for president.

1973   Audre Lorde: *From a Land Where Other People Live; Chattanooga*; Alice Walker: *Revolutionary Petunias & Other Poems*; Nikki Giovanni: Ego *Tripping and Other Poems for Young Children*; Sonia Sanchez: *Love Poems and A Blues Book for Blue Black Magical Women* and *Says Jerome*; Mari Evans: *JD*; William Waring Cuney: *Storefront Church*; Frank John: *Light a Fire*.

1974   Ishmael Reed: *The Last Days of Louisiana Red; An Ordinary Woman*; Mari Evans: *I Look at Me!*

1974   Amiri Baraka urges Congress of African People to emphasize class struggle over racial differences.

1975   Amiri Baraka: *Hard Facts*; Audre Lorde: *New York Head Shop and Museum*; Maya Angelou: *Oh Pray My Wings Are Going to Fit Me Well*; Nikki Giovanni: *The Women and the Men*; Carolyn Rodgers: *How I Got Ovah: New and Selected Poems*; Ntozake Shange: *for colored girls who have considered suicide/when the rainbow is enuf*; Anne Williams: *Peacock Poems*; Paulette White: *Love Poem to a Black Junkie*.

1976   Audre Lorde: *Between Ourselves and Coal*; Ishmael Reed: *Flight to Canada*; Ntozake Shange: *Melissa & Smith*; Maya Angelou: *And Still I Rise*; Lucille Clifton: *Generations*; Jay Wright: *Dimensions of History* and *Soothsayers and Omens*.

1977   Ntozake Shange: *Natural Disasters and Other Festive Occasions*; Michael S. Harper: *Images of Kin: New and Selected Poems*; Rita Dove: *Ten Poems*.

1978   Audre Lorde: *The Black Unicorn*; Ishmael Reed: *A Secretary to the Spirits; Shrovetide in Old New Orleans*; Ntozake Shange: *Nappy Edges*; Nikki Giovanni: *Cotton Candy on a Rainy Day*;

Sonia Sanchez: *I've Been a Women*; Carolyn Rodgers: *The Heart as Ever Green.*

1979   *Selected Poetry of Amiri Baraka/Leroi Jones* and *The Sidney Poet Historical*; Alice Walker: *Good Night, Willie Lee, I'll See You in the Morning*; Mari Evans: *Jim Flying High.*

1980   Nikki Giovanni: *Vacation Time; Poems for Children*; Jay Wright: *The Double Invention o f Komo.*

1981   Amiri Baraka: *reggae or not!*; Randall Dudley: *A Litany of Friends: New and Selected Poems.*

1982   Audre Lorde: *Chosen Poems;* Ishmael Reed: *The Terrible Twos;* Gloria Naylor: *The Women of Brewster Place*; Ntozake Shange: *Sassafrass, Cypress, and Indigo.*

1983   Alice Walker wins Pulitzer Prize for Fiction and the American Book Award for *The Color Purple*; Gloria Naylor wins the American Book Award for *The Women of Brewster Place.*

1983   Ntozake Shange: *A Daughter's Geography*; Rita Dove: *Museum*; Raymond R. Patterson: *Elemental Blues: Poems 1981–1982.*

1984   Ntozake Shange: *From Okra to Greens*; Alice Walker: *Horses Make a Landscape Look More Beautiful*; Jay Wright: *Explications/Interpretations.*

1985   *The Poetry and Poetics of Amiri Baraka: The Jazz Aesthetic.*

1986   Audre Lorde: *Our Dead Behind Us*; Ishmael Reed: *New and Collected Poems*; Rita Dove: *Thomas and Beulah.*

1987   Rita Dove wins Pulitzer Prize for Poetry for *Thomas and Beulah.*

1987   Ntozake Shange: *Ridin' the Moon in Texas: Word Paintings;* Samuel Allen: *Every Round and Other Poems.*

1988   Rita Dove: *The Other Side of the House*; Gloria Naylor: *Mama Day.*

1989   Ishmael Reed: *The Terrible Threes*; Rita Dove: *The Yellow House on the Corner*; Delores Kendrick: *Women of Plums: Poems in the Voices of Save Women.*

1990   Colleen McElroy: *What Madness Brought Me Here: Collected Poems, 1968–1988.*

1991   Lucille Clifton: *Quilting: Poems 1987–1990.*

1992	Mari Evans: *A Dark and Splendid Mass.*
1993	Rita Dove: *Through the Ivory Gate.*
1994	Rita Dove is the first African American to be named U.S. poet laureate. Yusef Komunyakaa is awarded the Pulitzer Prize for *Neon Vernacular: New and Selected Poems.*
1995	Rita Dove: *The Poet's World* and *Mother Love.*
1996	Rita Dove: *The Darker Face of the Earth.*
1999	Rita Dove: *On the Bus with Rosa Parks*; Sonia Sanchez: *Shake Loose My Skin: New and Selected Poems*; Calvin C. Hernton: *The Red Crab Gang* and *Black River Poems.*
2000	Michael S. Harper: *Songlines in Michaeltree: New and Collected Poems.* Lucile Clifton receives a National Book Award for *Blessing the Boats: New and Collected Poems 1988–2000.*
2001	Yusef Komunyakaa: *Pleasure Dome: New and Collected Poems*; Dolores Kendrick: *Why the Woman Is Singing on the Corner: A Verse Narrative.*
2005	Mari Evans: *Clarity as Concept: A Poet's Perspective.*
2006	Nathaniel Mackey receives the National Book Award for *Splay Anthem.*
2007	Natasha Trethewey is awarded the Pulitzer Prize for *Native Guard*, published the previous year.
2010	Lucille Clifton dies on February 13.

Contributors

HAROLD BLOOM is Sterling Professor of the Humanities at Yale University. Educated at Cornell and Yale universities, he is the author of more than 30 books, including *Shelley's Mythmaking* (1959), *The Visionary Company* (1961), *Blake's Apocalypse* (1963), *Yeats* (1970), *The Anxiety of Influence* (1973), *A Map of Misreading* (1975), *Kabbalah and Criticism* (1975), *Agon: Toward a Theory of Revisionism* (1982), *The American Religion* (1992), *The Western Canon* (1994), *Omens of Millennium: The Gnosis of Angels, Dreams, and Resurrection* (1996), *Shakespeare: The Invention of the Human* (1998), *How to Read and Why* (2000), *Genius: A Mosaic of One Hundred Exemplary Creative Minds* (2002), *Hamlet: Poem Unlimited* (2003), *Where Shall Wisdom Be Found?* (2004), and *Jesus and Yahweh: The Names Divine* (2005). In addition, he is the author of hundreds of articles, reviews, and editorial introductions. In 1999, Professor Bloom received the American Academy of Arts and Letters' Gold Medal for Criticism. He has also received the International Prize of Catalonia, the Alfonso Reyes Prize of Mexico, and the Hans Christian Andersen Bicentennial Prize of Denmark.

AUDREY T. McCLUSKEY began teaching English at Cleveland State University where she created and taught one of the first college courses on black women writers. She continued teaching classes on African-American literature and black women writers when she later took a position at Indiana University.

WILLIAM J. HARRIS was poetry editor for *Epoch* and *Sojourner* magazines, and his poetry and essays have been published in numerous anthologies. He has held teaching positions at Cornell University, University of California at Riverside, and SUNY at Stony Brook.

MAX W. THOMAS has contributed scholarly articles to publications including *The Iowa Review*.

ELIZABETH DODD directs the creative writing program and teaches in the English department at Kansas State University.

ZOFIA BURR teaches in the English department at George Mason University. She is also the editor of *Set in Motion: Essays, Interviews, and Dialogues* by A. R. Ammons.

MALIN PEREIRA teaches African-American and American literatures at the University of North Carolina at Charlotte.

ANGELA M. SALAS teaches in the English department at Clarke College in Dubuque, Iowa. She is also the author of *Race, Human Empathy, and Negative Capability* (2003).

JAMES SMETHURST teaches in the W.E.B. DuBois Department of Afro-American Studies at the University of Massachusetts in Amherst. His published work includes *The New Red Negro: The Literary Left and African-American Poetry, 1930–1946* (1999) and *The Black Arts Movement: Literary Nationalism in the 1960s and 1970s* (2005).

RICK BENJAMIN is a teacher of poetry and community practice at Brown University and the Rhode Island School of Design. His poetry has been published most recently in the journal *Watershed*. Benjamin is the state director of River of Words, an ecological educational program for grades K–12 and co-director of the Rhode Island Service Alliance.

ANNETTE DEBO is assistant professor and director of the literature program at Western Carolina University.

Bibliography

Selected Works by the Poets

Angelou, Maya. *Just Give Me a Cool Drink of Water 'fore I Diiie*. New York: Random House 1971.

———. *I Know Why the Caged Bird Sings*. 1970.

Baraka, Amiri. *Transbluency: The Selected Poems of Amiri Baraka / LeRoi Jones (1961–1995)*, Paul Vangelisti, ed. New York: Marsilio Publishers, 1995.

Clifton, Lucille. *Good News About the Earth*. New York: Random House, 1972.

———. *Generations*. New York: Random House, 1976.

———. *Everett Anderson's Christmas Coming*. New York: Holt, Rinehart, 1971.

———. *Some of the Days of Everett Anderson*. New York: Holt, Rinehart, 1970.

———. *Everett Anderson's Year*. New York: Holt, Rinehart, 1971.

———. *Good, Says Jerome*. New York: Dutton, 1973.

———. *The Black BC's*. New York: Dutton, 1970.

———. *An Ordinary Woman*. New York: Random House, 1974.

———. *Generations: A Memoir*. New York: Random House, 1976.

———. *Good Woman: Poems and a Memoir 1969–1980*. Brockport, NY: BOA Editions, Ltd., 1987.

———. *The Terrible Stories: Poems*. Brockport, NY: BOA Editions, Ltd., 1997.

Dove, Rita. *American Smooth*. New York: W. W. Norton, 2004.

———. *Grace Notes*. New York: W. W. Norton, 1989.

———. *Mother Love*. New York: W. W. Norton, 1995.

———. *Museum*. Pittsburgh: Carnegie Mellon University Press, 1986.

———. *On the Bus with Rosa Parks.* New York: W. W. Norton, 1999.

———. *Rita Dove: Selected Poems.* New York: Vintage Books, 1993.

———. *Sonata Mulattica.* New York: W. W. Norton, 2009.

———. *Thomas and Beulah.* Pittsburgh: Carnegie Mellon University Press, 1986.

———. *The Yellow House on the Corner.* Pittsburgh: Carnegie Mellon University Press, 1980.

Giovanni, Nikki. *Black Feeling Black Talk Black Judgement.* New York: William Morrow & Co., 1970.

———. *Black Judgement.* Detroit, Michigan: Broadside Press, 1971.

———. *Re: Creation.* Detroit Michigan: Broadside Press, 1970.

———. *This Is My House.* New York: William Morrow, 1972.

Harper, Michael S. *Dear John, Dear Coltrane.* Pittsburgh: University of Pittsburg Press, 1970.

———. *Debridement.* Garden City: Doubleday, 1973.

———. *History as Apple Tree.* San Francisco: Scareb, 1972.

———. *History Is Your Own Heartbeat.* Urbana: University of Illinois Press, 1971.

———. *Honorable Amendments.* Urbana: University of Illinois Press, 1995.

———. *Images of Kin: New and Selected Poems.* Urbana: University of Illinois Press, 1977.

———. *Nightmare Begins Responsibility.* Urbana: University of Illinois Press, 1975.

———. *Song: I Want a Witness.* Pittsburgh: University of Pittsburgh Press, 1972.

———. *Songlines in Michaeltree: New and Collected Poems.* Urbana: University of Illinois Press, 2000.

Komunyakaa, Yusef. *Dien Cai Dau.* Hanover: Wesleyan University Press, 1988.

———. *Magic City.* Hanover: Wesleyan University Press, 1992.

———. *Neon Vernacular: New and Selected Poems.* Hanover: Wesleyan University Press, 1993.

———. *Pleasure Dome: New and Collected Poems.* Middletown, CT: Wesleyan University Press, 2001.

———. *Talking Dirty to the Gods.* New York: Farrar, Straus & Giroux, 2000.

———. *Thieves of Paradise.* Hanover: Wesleyan University Press, 1998.

———. *Warhorses.* New York: Farrar, Straus & Giroux, 2009.

Lorde, Audre. *The First Cities.* New York: Poets Press, 1968.

———. *Black Unicorn.* New York: Norton, 1978.

———. *A Burst of Light: Essays.* Ithaca, NY: Firebrand Books, 1988.

———. *The Cancer Journals.* San Francisco: Spinsters / Aunt Lute, 1980.

———. *Chosen Poems: Old and New.* New York: Norton, 1982.

———. *The Marvelous Distance of Arithmetic.* New York: Norton, 1993.

————. *Undersong: Chosen Poems, Old and New.* Revised. New York: W. W. Norton, 1992.

————. *Zami: A New Spelling of My Name.* Freedom, CA: Crossing Press, 1982.

————. *Our Dead Behind Us: Poems.* New York and London: Norton, 1986.

————. *Apartheid U. S. A.* New York: Kitchen Table, 1985.

————. *Need: A Chorale for Black Women Voices.* Latham, NY: Kitchen Table, 1990.

————. *The Audre Lorde Compendium.* London: Pandora, 1996.

————. *The Collected Poems.* New York and London: Norton, 1997.

Phillips, Carl. *In the Blood.* Boston: Northeastern University Press, 1992.

————. *Cortege.* Saint Paul, MN: Graywolf, 1995.

————. *From the Devotions.* Saint Paul, MN: Graywolf, 1998.

————. *Pastoral.* Saint Paul, MN: Graywolf, 2000.

————. *The Tether.* New York: Farrar, Straus and Giroux, 2001.

————. *Rock Harbor.* New York: Farrar, Straus and Giroux, 2002.

————. *The Rest of Love.* New York: Farrar, Straus and Giroux, 2004

————. *Riding Westward.* New York: Farrar, Straus and Giroux, 2006.

————. *Quiver of Arrows: Selected Poems, 1986–2006.* New York: Farrar, Straus and Giroux, 2007.

————. *Speak Low.* New York: Farrar, Straus and Giroux, 2009.

Reed, Ishmael. *The Free-lance Pallbearers.* Garden City, NY: Doubleday, 1967.

————. *Yellow Back Radio Broke-Down.* Garden City, NY: Doubleday, 1969.

————. *catechism of d neoamerican hoodoo church.* London: P. Breman, 1971.

————. *Conjure: Selected Poems, 1963–1970.* Amherst: University of Massachusetts Press, 1972.

————. *Mumbo Jumbo.* Garden City, New York: Doubleday, 1972.

————. *Chattanooga: Poems.* New York: Random House, 1973.

————. *The Last Days of Louisiana Red.* New York: Random House, 1974.

————. *Flight to Canada.* New York: Random House, 1976.

————. *A Secretary to the Spirits.* New York: NOK, 1978.

————. *Shrovetide in Old New Orleans.* Garden City, NY: Doubleday, 1978.

————. *God Made Alaska for the Indians: Selected Essays.* NY: Garland, 1982.

————. *The Terrible Twos.* New York: St. Martin's Press / Marek, 1982.

————. *Cab Calloway Stands in for the Moon.* Flint, Michigan: Bamberger, 1986.

————. *Reckless Eyeballing.* New York: St. Martin's Press, 1986.

————. *New and Collected Poems.* New York: Atheneum, 1988.

————. *Writin' Is Fightin': Thirty-seven Years of Boxing on Paper.* New York: Atheneum, 1988.

———. *The Terrible Threes.* New York: Atheneum, 1989.

———. *The Reed Reader.* New York: Basic Books, 2000.

———. *Blues City: a Walk in Oakland.* New York: Crown Journeys, 2003.

Sanchez, Sonia. *Home Coming.* Detroit: Broadside: 1969.

———. *We BaddDDD People.* Detroit: Broadside Press, 1970.

———. *A Blues Book for Blue Black Magical Women.* Detroit: Broadside, 1973.

Shange, Ntozake. *for colored girls who have considered suicide when the raindbow is enuf: a choreopoem.* New York: Collier-MacMillan Company, 1977.

———. *nappy edges.* New York: St. Martin's Press, 1978.

———. *The Love Space Demands.* New York: St. Martin's Press, 1991.

Trethewey, Natasha. *Domestic Work.* Saint Paul, MN: Graywolf, 2000.

———. *Bellocq's Ophelia: Poems.* Saint Paul, MN: Graywolf, 2002.

———. *Native Guard.* New York: Houghton Mifflin/Mariner, 2006.

Wright, Jay. *The Homecoming Singer.* New York: Corinth Books, 1971.

———. *The Dimensions of History.* Santa Cruz, CA: Kayak, 1976.

———. *Selected Poems of Jay Wright*, Robert B. Stepto, ed. Princeton, NJ: Princeton University Press, 1987.

———. *Soothsayers and Omens.* New York: Seven Woods Press. 1976.

Young, Kevin. *Black Maria.* New York: Knopf, 2005.

———. *For the Confederate Dead.* New York: Knopf, 2007.

———. *jelly roll.* New York: Knopf, 2003.

———. *Most Way Home.* Hanover, NH: Zoland, 2000.

———. *To Repel Ghosts.* South Royalton, VT: Zoland, 2001.

Works about the Poets

Armbruster, Karla, and Kathleen R. Wallace, eds. *Beyond Nature Writing: Expanding the Boundaries of Ecocriticism.* Charlottesville and London: University Press of Virginia, 2001.

Bolden, Tony. *Afro-Blue: Improvisations in African American Poetry and Culture.* Urbana and Chicago: University of Illinois Press, 2004.

Bowles, Gloria, M., Giulia Fabi, and Arlene R. Keizer, eds. *New Black Feminist Criticism, 1985–2000 / Barbara Christian.* Urbana and Chicago: University of Illinois Press, 2007.

Burr, Zofia. *Of Women, Poetry, and Power: Strategies of Address in Dickinson, Miles, Brooks, Lorde, and Angelou.* Urbana and Chicago: University of Illinois Press, 2002.

Christian, Barbara. *Black Feminist Criticism: Perspectives on Black Women Writers.* New York, Oxford, Beijing, Frankfurt, Sao Paulo, Sydney, Tokyo, Toronto: Pergamon Press, 1985.

Clarke, Cheryl. *"After Mecca": Women Poets and the Black Arts Movement.* New Brunswick, New Jersey, and London: Rutgers University Press, 2005.

Collins, Lisa Gail, and Margo Natalie Crawford, eds. *New Thoughts on the Black Arts Movement.* New Brunswick, New Jersey, and London: Rutgers University Press, 2006.

Evans, Mari, ed. *Black Women Writers: 1950–1980.* New York: Double Day, Anchor Books, 1984.

Gabbin, Joanne Veal, ed. *Shaping Memories: Reflections of African American Women Writers.* Jackson: University Press of Mississippi, 2009.

Gates, Henry Louis, Jr. *The Signifying Monkey: A Theory of African-American Literary Criticism.* New York and Oxford: Oxford University Press, 1985.

———, ed. *Black Literature and Literary Theory.* New York and London: Methuen: 1984.

Hudson, Theodore R. *From LeRoi Jones to Amiri Baraka: The Literary Works.* Durham, North Carolina: Duke University Press. 1973.

Ingersoll, Earl G., ed. *Conversations with Rita Dove.* Jackson: University Press of Mississippi, 2003.

Keating, AnaLouise. *Women Reading / Women Writing.* Philadelphia: Temple University Press, 1996.

Mance, Ajuan Maria. *Inventing Black Women: African American Women Poets and Self-Representation, 1877–2000.* Knoxville: The University of Tennessee Press, 2007.

Martin, Reginald. *Ishmael Reed and the New Black Aesthetic Critics.* New York: St. Martin's Press, 1988.

Mitchell, Angelyn, and Danille K. Taylor, eds. *African American Women's Literature.* Cambridge: Cambridge University Press, 2009.

Nielsen, Aldon Lynn, ed. *Reading Race in American Poetry: "An Area of Act."* Urbana and Chicago: University of Illinois Press, 2000.

Pereira, Malin. *Rita Dove's Cosmopolitanism.* Urbana and Chicago: University of Illinois Press, 2003.

Ramey, Laurie, ed. *The Heritage Series of Black Poetry, 1962–1975: A Research Compendium.* Hampshire, England: Ashgate Publishing Limited, 2008.

Rankine, Claudia, and Lisa Sewell, eds. *American Poets in the 21st Century: The New Poetics.* Middleton, Connecticut: Wesleyan University Press, 2007.

Righelato, Pat. *Understanding Rita Dove.* Columbia: University of South Carolina Press, 2006.

Tate, Claudia, ed. *Black Women Writers at Work.* New York: The Continuum Publishing Company, 1983.

Watts, Jerry Gafio. *Amiri Baraka: The Politics and Art of a Black Intellectual.* New York and London: New York University Press, 2001.

Acknowledgments

Audrey T. McCluskey. "Tell the Good News: A View of the Works of Lucille Clifton." From *Black Women Writers (1950–1980): A Critical Evaluation*, edited by Mari Evans. Published by Anchor Books/Doubleday. Copyright © 1984 by Mari Evans. Used by permission of Doubleday, a division of Random House, Inc.

William J. Harris. "Sweet Soft Essence of Possibility: The Poetry of Nikki Giovanni." From *Black Women Writers (1950–1980): A Critical Evaluation*, edited by Mari Evans. Published by Anchor Books/Doubleday. Copyright © 1984 by Mari Evans. Used by permission of Doubleday, a division of Random House, Inc.

Max W. Thomas. "Mighty Lines." *The Iowa Review*, vol. 30, no. 2 (Fall 2000). Copyright © 2000 *The Iowa Review*.

Elizabeth Dodd. "The Great Rainbow Swamp: History as Moral Ecology in the Poetry of Michael S. Harper." From *Beyond Nature Writing: Expanding the Boundaries of Ecocriticism*, edited by Karla M. Armbruster and Kathleen R. Wallace, pp. 177–94. Copyright © 2001 by the Rector and Visitors of the University of Virginia. Reprinted by permission of the University of Virginia Press.

Zofia Burr. "Maya Angelou and the Inaugural Stage." From *Of Women, Poetry, and Power: Strategies of Address in Dickinson, Miles, Brooks, Lorde, and Angelou*. Copyright © 2002 by Board of Trustees of the University of Illinois. Used with permission if the University of Illinois Press.

179

Malin Pereira, *"Museum* and Cosmopolitanism." From *Rita Dove's Cosmopolitanism*. Copyright © 2003 by Board of Trustees of the University of Illinois. Used with permission if the University of Illinois Press.

Angela M. Salas, "Human Empathy and Negative Capability: Yusef Komunyakaa's Poetry." From *Flashback Through the Heart: The Poetry of Yusef Komunyakaa*. Published by Susquehanna University Press/Associated University Presses. Copyright © 2004 by Rosemont Publishing and Printing.

James Smethurst, "The Black Arts Movement and Historically Black Colleges and Universities." From *New Thoughts on the Black Arts Movement*, edited by Lisa Gail Collins and Margo Natalie Crawford. Copyright © 2006 by Rutgers, the State University. Reprinted by permission of Rutgers University Press.

Rick Benjamin, "Mixed-Up Medium: Kevin Young's Turn-of-the-Century American Triptych." From *American Poets in the 21st Century: The New Poetics*, edited by Claudia Rankine and Lisa Sewell. Copyright © 2007 by Rick Benjamin and reprinted by permission of Wesleyan University Press.

Annette Debo, "Opheila Speaks: Resurrecting Still Lives in Natasha Trethewey's *Bellocq's Ophelia*." *African American Review* vol. 42 no. 2 (Summer 2008). Copyright © 2008 Annette Debo.

Index